The Authors

Maralene and Miles Wesner are multi-talented teachers and prolific writers. They have published more than 150 Audio-Visual Education aids, and pioneered new reading methods with their Phonics in a Nutshell (1965).

They have written articles, and mission studies for Southern Baptist periodicals. They were in the original group of writers to develop WMU's Big "A" Club material.

They've published several books with Broadman Press: *A Fresh Look at the Gospel* (1983); *You Are What You Choose* (1984); and *How To Be a Saint When You Feel Like a Sinner* (1986) and self-published 30 books by Diversity Press.

They are noted for their no-nonsense style, their clear illustrations, and their willingness to face controversial issues. From the dual perspectives of both academic and religious professions, they seek to be a bridge between the spiritual and the intellectual worlds.

They hold Masters Degrees (MEd) from Oklahoma University plus work toward a Doctorate. Miles also attended Southwestern Baptist Theological Seminary, and served as a high school counselor. He has been the bi-vocational pastor of a small rural church for more than 50 years.

Both Maralene and Miles taught in public school and collages and served as educational consultants. Maralene taught Psychology and Speech for Southeastern Oklahoma State University for 32 years. She was chosen Oklahoma Teacher of the Year in 1975.

They have planned, led tours, and done research in all of the 50 states, Canada, Mexico, Europe, Egypt, Japan, and the Holy Land. In 1985, they were among a small group of Americans who were invited by Dr. Joseph P. Kennedy of the US/China Education Foundation and Bishop Ting, leader of the Three Self Movement, to participate in the First Symposium on the Church in Nanjing, China.

Now, they use their lifetime of varied experiences to write insightful sermons, essays, and books.

Titles by Maralene & Miles Wesner
published by Nurturing Faith

Sermons for Special Days

Life More Abundant

Do You Really Know Jesus?

If Jesus Were Here Today

IF *Jesus* WERE HERE TODAY

Maralene & Miles Wesner

© 2022
Published in the United States by Nurturing Faith, Macon, GA.
Nurturing Faith is a book imprint of Good Faith Media (goodfaithmedia.org).
Library of Congress Cataloging-in-Publication Data is available.

ISBN: 978-1-63528-186-6

All rights reserved. Printed in the United States of America.

Scripture quotations are from New Revised Standard Version Bible, copyright © 1989 National Council of the Churches of Christ in the United States of America. Used by permission. All rights reserved worldwide.

Cover photograph by David Cassady.

Contents

Preface 1
1. Jesus Makes an Important Commitment 3
2. Jesus Endures a Period of Temptation 7
3. Jesus Chooses Twelve Diverse Helpers 11
4. Jesus Accepts a Dysfunctional Woman 15
5. Jesus Uses a Child's Lunch 21
6. Jesus Defends a Fallen Woman 27
7. Jesus Enables a Traitor to Change 33
8. Jesus Confronts a Vengeful Mob 39
9. Jesus Deals with Ambitious Disciples 43
10. Jesus Emphasizes Forgiveness 49
11. Jesus Commands Tolerance and Concern 55
12. Jesus Describes a Rebellious Son 61
13. Jesus Rebukes a Selfish Miser 65
14. Jesus Warns About Self-Righteousness 69
15. Jesus Gives Advice about Productivity 75
16. Jesus Encourages the Use of Opportunities 79
17. Jesus Finally Loses His Temper 83
18. Jesus Faces a Personal Crisis 89
19. Jesus Offers Reconciliation 95

Preface

Jesus's life in Palestine was drastically different from our life in America. However, as Christians we're expected to emulate his beliefs and actions. Trying to discover and salvage the true character and message of Jesus from the Gospels is a real challenge. Nevertheless, we can study the Gospels and extrapolate the truth from these stories.

It's difficult to know the mind and follow the example of a person who lived so long ago, but the Gospels do include some frequently overlooked vignettes that teach us about Jesus's personal character, values, and methods of ministry. They can help us determine what Jesus would say and do about current issues.

Jesus was an extremely practical individual. For instance, when John the Baptist questioned Jesus about his identity and position of authority, he didn't quote scriptural prophecy. He didn't present complicated theological arguments. He didn't even react with an emotional defense. Instead, he simply instructed him to examine the evidence (see Matt 11:2–5). Over and over, he used logic to make his point or win his argument.

This is a simple method all of us can still use today. If a traditional religious practice or doctrine leads to confusion or harmful consequences, then it should be discarded. Considering these and other seemingly insignificant incidents allows us glimpses into Jesus's attitudes, thinking patterns, and techniques of operation. This will enable us to discover a common-sense gospel that we can accept and apply in our modern world.

Chapter 1

Jesus Makes an Important Commitment

In order for Jesus to become real to us, we must get him out of white robes, take him off the donkey, and let him live in the context of our modern culture. Obsolete terms and conditions blunt the impact of the gospel. If our lives are to be affected, we must bring the message of Jesus into the twenty-first century. We must discover what Jesus would say and do if he lived in America today instead of in Palestine two thousand years ago.

As time passes, basic human needs and feelings remain the same. It's only the language and technology that change. So let's use our spiritual imagination to re-create some events and teachings of the gospel. Let's consider how Jesus might respond to them if they were occurring today.

One person can really make a difference, and Jesus was such a person. Most divine figures have fanciful legends describing their earthly entrance. But Jesus came into this world the same way we all do. He was raised in the home of ordinary, working-class parents. Even as a young boy, Jesus did things that upset his family. His growth was normal in every way.

Jesus made one of his first important spiritual decisions when he went to hear his cousin John the Baptist. We don't know exactly why Jesus was attracted to John's crusade. He might have responded because of the evangelist's powerful personality. The scriptures record his strange behavior, saying, "John was clothed with camel's hair, with a leather belt around his waist, and he ate locusts and wild honey" (Mark 1:6).

Jesus might have responded because of John's blunt language and straight talk. He pulled no punches. When the crowds came out to be baptized by him, John said, "You brood of vipers! Who warned you to flee from the wrath to come? Bear fruits worthy of repentance. Do not begin to say to yourselves, 'We have Abraham as our ancestor'; for I tell you, God is able from these stones to raise up children to Abraham. Even now the ax is lying at the root of the trees; every tree therefore that does not bear good fruit is cut down and thrown into the fire" (Luke 3:7–9).

Jesus probably responded because John presented practical doctrines with an emphasis on human welfare. Jesus approved John's common-sense moral principles. Whatever the reason, Jesus responded to John's message and "was baptized by John in the Jordan" (Mark 1:9).

Why do you suppose Jesus felt the need to take this important step? What lessons can we learn from this event? First, Jesus's baptism identified him with ordinary people. Jesus never tried to put himself above others. In fact, he criticized those who did. Not only that, but it placed him squarely in the company of sinners.

If Jesus were here today, we would still expect him to identify with common people. He wouldn't identify himself with the country club set or the political VIPs or even the well-known religious leaders. Instead, he would associate with farmers and mechanics and teachers and housewives. He would even associate with those who are socially "undesirable": maybe Las Vegas showgirls, ex-convicts, or impious agnostics.

Jesus was often criticized for such behavior. In his day, eating with someone meant accepting them as equals. Tax collectors were "traitors," who worked for the enemy and stole from their fellow citizens; "sinners" included prostitutes and religious rebels. These are the people Jesus associated with.

Next, Jesus's baptism enabled him to make a public commitment. This important event connected him with righteousness and justice. It provided an opportunity for him to take a stand on a crucial issue. John's theology emphasized moral actions rather than traditional rituals, and this became a distinguishing theme of Jesus's own message.

If Jesus were here today, he would still take a stand on social issues. He would still dedicate himself to personal morality. We don't know what particular denomination Jesus would join, but we do know he would be on the side of compassion and generosity. Jesus would be on the side of honesty. He would be on the side of those who oppose violence and greed.

Finally, Jesus's baptism gave him a support group. We know Jesus didn't necessarily agree with everything John preached because he soon branched off from John's movement. Nevertheless, at this point it was better than the alternative religions. In fact, Jesus chose many of his followers from this group of seekers.

If Jesus were here today, he would still realize that none of us can stand alone. Those who say they can be good Christians without a church affiliation are not following Jesus's example. He had people around him who could help with his ministry.

Jesus was a familiar figure. To his Nazareth neighbors, he was just the guy next door. He had absolutely no physical traits that stood out—no halo, no wings, no auras. Indeed, when some suggested he might be special, those who grew up with him protested: "Is not this the carpenter's son? Is not his mother called Mary? And are not his brothers James and Joseph and Simon and Judas? And are not all his sisters with us?" (Matt 13:55–56).

Some lives seem to leave no impression. They are like a hand that's pulled from a bucket of water. When it is withdrawn, the liquid closes in and no one would know it had ever been there. Other lives leave such an impression that it takes years, decades, and even centuries for their influence to be erased. A few leave a legacy that can never be erased. Jesus lived such a life.

Of course, Jesus's speech, dress, and travel would be different if he lived in America today. But he would still identify with common people; he would still take a stand on social issues; he would still seek out a support group. His basic responses concerning important commitments would still be the same.

Chapter 2

Jesus Endures a Period of Temptation

A little boy who lived near a lake had been warned never to go swimming alone. One day, his father caught him in the water. The little guy immediately protested, "But, Daddy, I didn't mean to go swimming. It just happened."

His father inquired, "Then why did you bring your swimsuit with you when you came here to play?"

The little boy answered, "Oh, I brought it along just in case I got tempted."

All of us "get" tempted. This forces us to make important value choices. These temptations may involve physical, moral, or spiritual issues. Jesus didn't get to avoid any of our human problems. After his public commitment and baptism, he immediately faced some major decisions. He spent forty days and forty nights in the wilderness, fasting and avoiding temptation (see Matt 4:1–10).

It's significant that these temptations came immediately after his greatest spiritual affirmation. That's something we can expect. After wonderful spiritual experiences, there's always a time of doubt and depression. Jesus was alone and exhausted and hungry. It's at such weak moments that we're apt to stumble. Satan tried to instill doubt, beginning each encounter with the words "*If* you are the Son of God." Jesus had just been assured of his status, and he was filled with the Holy Spirit. Still, these spiritual assurances didn't protect him from temptation. In fact, as long as he was on earth, he met temptations and faced human problems.

Why do you suppose these particular decisions occurred right at the beginning of his ministry? What lessons can we learn from this account? What point does it make about temptation?

First, the temptations dealt with physical needs. Fortunately, Jesus rose above instant gratification. If Jesus were here today, he would still put spiritual priorities over physical priorities. He would never become so materialistic that *things* would take precedence over integrity. He wouldn't try to "keep up with the Joneses." He wouldn't incur debt to buy expensive luxuries. He wouldn't elevate possessions over people.

Next, the temptations dealt with moral and emotional needs. Jesus was beginning to realize the magnitude of his mission. He felt called to carry out a momentous task. But he was an unknown figure in an obscure part of the world, with no connections in high places. How on earth could he influence anyone? Scripture says, "The devil took him to the holy city and placed him on the pinnacle of the temple, saying to him, 'If you are the Son of God, throw yourself down; for it is written, "He will command his angels concerning you," and "On their hands they will bear you up, so that you will not dash your foot against a stone"'" (Matt 4:5–6).

Now, this challenge was not based on a lie. The psalmist had promised that God would protect his anointed (see Ps 91:9–12). But Jesus realized the danger of cherry-picking scriptures for our own benefit and answered, "Again it is written, 'Do not put the Lord your God to the test'" (Matt 4:7).

If Jesus were here today, he would still reject the use of gimmicks. He wouldn't claim supernatural miracles. He wouldn't use advertising hype. He wouldn't resort to emotional scare tactics. In fact, he often avoided publicity. Many times, he even warned his disciples not to emphasize supernatural powers (see Matt 16:20; Mark 8:30; 9:9; Luke 5:14; 8:56). He knew people who respond to novelty and excitement will fall away as soon as the excitement fades. Some of the same individuals who yelled "Hosanna!" at his triumphant entry into Jerusalem probably yelled "Crucify!" that Friday.

Finally, the temptations dealt with spiritual needs. When Jesus considered the problems of the world and his own earthly limitations, the challenge seemed impossible. He probably wondered if a compromise with the world might be necessary. Perhaps he thought, "Maybe if I cooperated with the power structures, I'd have more clout." But Jesus reacted decisively to such temptation.

If Jesus were here today, he would still avoid immoral shortcuts. He wouldn't sell out to powerful institutions. He wouldn't compromise with evil.

It's notable that none of Jesus's temptations involved overt sins. That's still true of us. Few believers are really tempted to murder or commit adultery or steal. Instead, we're tempted to make excuses, neglect worship, slander a competitor, or pad our expense account.

Unfortunately, compromising with sin is a slippery slope. No garden *suddenly* becomes overgrown with weeds. No building *suddenly* crumbles. No person *suddenly* becomes a criminal. It's usually a gradual process that starts with small temptations.

Once, a minister called a boy from the audience and tied his hands together with a little piece of thread. It was easy for the boy to break loose. When he wound the thread three times, it was harder to break. Soon, so many threads bound the boy's hands together that he was helpless. Sin is like that thread. It looks so harmless at first, but eventually it makes us prisoners!

Now, if this were today, would Jesus be tempted to use his personal abilities in order to gain financial security? Would he be tempted to use dramatic gimmicks to get media coverage and attract attention? Would he be tempted to compromise his message or use televangelism methods in order to gain fame? We don't know what form Jesus's temptations would take, but we know they would be real.

In fact, like all of us, he would have to face some situations that have no "right" answers. Can you imagine Jesus on election day, having to vote for one of two very flawed candidates? Would he speed if he were late for an appointment? Would he ever break one law to keep a higher law? What would he do if his retirement funds were invested in tobacco stocks?

Even though Jesus would have to deal with different issues if he lived in America today, his basic response about facing temptations would remain the same.

Chapter 3

Jesus Chooses Twelve Diverse Helpers

A disgusted CEO once said, "A leader has to decide what needs to be done and tell somebody to do it. Later, he discovers it hasn't been done and must listen to excuses from the person who should have done it. Finally, the leader realizes that he could have done the job himself in ten minutes instead of spending three weeks trying to find out why somebody else did it wrong ."

Depending on other people can be frustrating. Even so, it's impossible to do everything alone. We must learn to delegate. We must develop teamwork skills. Jesus knew he needed help to carry out his mission, and he carefully selected a group of associates. Some of the men responded, but many didn't.

One of the saddest rejections came from the rich young ruler (see Mark 10:17–22). Jesus saw potential in this talented young seeker. He had a special personal affinity for him, but he let him walk away. He didn't try to persuade him with promises of reward. He didn't threaten him with dire punishments. He didn't try to manipulate him with guilt or fear. He just let him go. Jesus never pressured anyone! In fact, he even discouraged some overzealous would-be followers because he felt they were responding without realizing the seriousness of their commitment.

The Gadarene demoniac, whom Jesus healed, begged to follow but was given a different assignment. Others who were invited made excuses. Eventually, out of the crowds of people, Jesus selected twelve men to be his close associates. He organized a group that corresponded symbolically to the twelve tribes of Israel. Jesus needed twelve normal individuals; twelve geniuses would not have been useful. He knew his future mission would be successful only if ordinary men and women were able to carry it out.

Jesus chose people with diverse backgrounds and abilities. Some in his group were leaders; some were followers. They were different in temperament, age, and aptitude. They came from different geographical areas and different economic brackets. Five were fishermen and businessmen. At least one belonged to a radical political faction, and one was an educated government appointee. Even their belief systems were radically different. Jesus never demanded uniformity; he always demanded authenticity.

If Jesus were here today, he would still need people with various abilities. Our communication methods are not like those of first-century Palestine. We are an electronic and technological society. He would have to consider people with media expertise and computer literacy. Our teachers and writers and communicators have to use modern techniques. Formal education would be much more important. Also, to reach a wider world, he would need men and women who speak different languages and understand different cultures. Jesus would need to choose a diverse group of helpers.

Jesus chose people who were willing to learn and serve. He was beginning a new venture. He was advocating drastic changes, and change is always resisted. The educated theologians and priests and religious leaders were already conditioned to the old ways. Their minds were set on certain outlooks and beliefs and practices. They had a vested interest in the status quo. They were the ones who rejected his message. Those who think they already know aren't teachable.

If Jesus were here today, he would still want people who are open to new ideas. Jesus's ideology was absolutely opposite to the traditional doctrines and worship practices of his day. This is one of the most unrecognized characteristics of his movement. He literally overturned the beliefs and customs of the orthodox religious institutions. If he wanted to make radical changes in beliefs and customs, he could not use people who are set in their ways and adamant about specific doctrines. He could not work with fanatics. Jesus would need to choose open-minded volunteers.

Jesus chose people with potential. These men were not especially religious, but Jesus knew they had valuable personal traits that could be developed. Peter was a crude fisherman, but Jesus saw qualities of strength and initiative and said, "'You are Simon son of John. You are to be called Cephas (which, is translated Peter)" (John 1:42). This new name meant "rock," and Peter became a strong leader.

James and John were so high-tempered and impulsive that Jesus gave them a humorous nickname: "Boanerges, that is, Sons of Thunder" (see Mark 3:17). They were also arrogant and vengeful. When they asked for positions of authority, the incident caused jealousy and conflict among the other disciples. Such dissension was common. The members of this group often argued among themselves.

Matthew, a despised tax collector, became a Gospel writer. Jesus chose Matthew, a social outcast, and he had the skills needed to record Jesus's life and teachings.

All in all, Jesus's disciples may have had questionable qualifications. Even so, these flawed men became Jesus's trusted friends, and they would eventually spread the gospel to the whole world. Jesus chose people with the potential to adapt to circumstances.

If Jesus were here today, he would still see value in some very unlikely people. His choices would probably surprise us and even irritate us. It's significant that he didn't include a single person from the orthodox religious establishment in his original group. Instead, he called ordinary people with weaknesses and faults. It's important to note that all of his disciples were normal individuals with personal problems. None were particularly pious. Peter was a foul-mouthed liar. James and John were hot-headed and ambitious. Thomas was a practical doubter. Matthew was a cunning politician. Nathaniel was a sarcastic cynic. Nevertheless, all of these men were willing to leave the past behind. They were willing to listen and learn. They were willing to change. That's essential!

Now, if this were today, would Jesus hire some secretaries, webmasters, and associate ministers, or would he persuade a group of faithful volunteers to work for free? Would Jesus recruit people from various denominations, or would he seek those who have been successful in secular positions? Would the group include a wide range of ages, races, and nationalities? Would he include women?

We don't know exactly whom Jesus would pick because the world is very different now. Jesus's associates today might include those from the secular and business and scientific fields. The original twelve worked at non-religious jobs before their call. Orthodoxy was not important. Concern and dedication were!

Jesus would still accept people as they are and try to bring out their strengths. A good leader inspires people to believe in him. A great leader inspires people to believe in themselves. Jesus did both.

Eleven of those twelve disciples faithfully discharged their responsibilities. Today, there's no one left to carry on his mission except us.

Even though Jesus would need people with contemporary skills if he lived in America today, he would still choose people with various backgrounds and abilities. He would still choose people with open minds who are willing to learn and serve.

Chapter 4

Jesus Accepts a Dysfunctional Woman

A poet said, "Please don't condemn the man who limps or stumbles down the road, unless you've worn the shoes he wears and borne his heavy load." Unfortunately, too many religions condemn those who are "different." Jesus demonstrated the very opposite attitude.

Most Jewish travelers took a detour to avoid Samaria. They detested these people, and the hostility was mutual. But Jesus wasn't a bigot. When a Samaritan woman came to draw water, "Jesus said to her, 'Give me a drink'" (John 4:7). This woman knew immediately that he was a Jew and was shocked that he even spoke to her: "'How is it that you, a Jew, ask a drink of me, a woman of Samaria?' Jesus answered her, 'If you knew the gift of God, and who it is that is saying to you, "Give me a drink," you would have asked him, and he would have given you living water.' The woman said to him, 'Sir, you have no bucket, and the well is deep. Where do you get that living water?'" (John 4:9–12).

Like most people, the woman thought only in literal terms. She wanted physical water. But Jesus offered spiritual renewal. He answered, "'Everyone who drinks of this water will be thirsty again, but those who drink of the water that I will give them will never be thirsty. The water that I will give will become in them a spring of water gushing up to eternal life.' The woman said to him, 'Sir, give me this water, so that I may never be thirsty or have to keep coming here to draw water'" (John 4:13–15).

She obviously didn't fully understand his explanation, but she was willing to accept what he had to offer. But now Jesus began to deal with more personal issues: "'Go, call your husband, and come back.' The woman answered him, 'I have no husband.' Jesus said to her, 'You are right in saying, "I have no husband"; for you have had five husbands, and the one you have now is not your husband'" (John 4:16–18).

There was no condemnation or shame in this statement. He simply acknowledged her predicament. Again, she was honest and open. She didn't defend herself or protest innocence. Instead, she asked a religious question: "Sir, I see that you are a prophet. Our ancestors worshiped on this mountain, but you say that the place where people must worship is in Jerusalem" (John 4:19–20).

Jesus expressed one of the deepest and most significant concepts of his entire ministry, surprisingly, to a woman (an immoral, pagan woman at that): "Woman, believe me, the hour is coming when you will worship the Father neither on this mountain nor in Jerusalem.... True worshipers will worship the Father in spirit and truth, for the Father seeks such as these to worship him. God is spirit, and those who worship him must worship in spirit and truth'" (John 4:21, 23–24).

He respected her, and she responded, "I know that Messiah is coming (who is called Christ). When he comes, he will proclaim all things to us" (John 4:25). Then he revealed his identity: "I am he, the one who is speaking to you" (John 4:26).

His disciples returned about this time and were shocked to see Jesus talking to this woman. They weren't as tolerant as he was, but they knew enough to keep quiet about it. Jesus's acceptance accomplished a wonderful transformation in this woman.

Why do you suppose Jesus interacted with this person in the way he did? What lessons can we learn from this incident? What point does he make about acceptance? First, Jesus wasn't concerned about her gender. In that day males didn't converse with females. They certainly didn't discuss theology, and they absolutely wouldn't do something as intimate as sharing a drink. But Jesus was not a chauvinist. He saw people as individual souls. He never made a distinction in his concern for men and women.

If Jesus were here today, he would still treat both males and females with respect. He would not categorize certain interests and abilities and occupations by gender. He was centuries ahead of the women's rights movement. He complimented Mary's interest in theology and scolded Martha for trying to keep her in "her place" as a servant in the kitchen. Jesus would see each person as a unique individual. He would realize that we are living in the time Joel (and later Peter) mentioned (see Acts 2:17–18).

Next, Jesus wasn't concerned about the woman's race. Samaritans were considered low-class half-breeds. Jews had absolutely no contact or interaction with them. But Jesus had an important conversation with this foreigner. In fact, he shared some of his deepest insights with her.

If Jesus were here today, he would still treat all racial and ethnic groups with respect. He would not assume every person of Middle Eastern descent is a terrorist. He would not claim that "God doesn't hear the prayers of Jews." He wouldn't discriminate against African Americans or Latinos or other minority groups. Instead, he would value the diverse talents and strengths and traditions of all human beings. His attitude inspired Peter to say, "I truly understand that God shows no partiality, but in every nation anyone who fears him and does what is right is acceptable to him" (Acts 10:34–35).

Finally, Jesus wasn't concerned about the woman's specific doctrinal beliefs. Samaritans had different customs and worship practices. Jesus didn't deal with any of those issues. He was not dogmatic about traditions and doctrinal purity. He valued every person. He never made a difference in his concern for orthodox or unorthodox creeds.

If Jesus were here today, he would still treat people of all belief systems with respect. Too many people say, "If you don't belong to my denomination, you can't take Communion with me"; "If you're not baptized as I prescribe, your baptism is no good"; "If your skin is not the color of mine, you cannot worship in my church." But there's really only one criterion: "By this everyone will know that you are my disciples, if you have love for one another" (John 13:35).

Accepting others is basic. At that time, there was a doctrinal argument about whether it was sinful to eat meat that had been associated with idols. Paul advised, "Some believe in eating anything, while the weak eat only vegetables. Those who eat must not despise those who abstain, and those who abstain must not pass judgment on those who eat; for God has welcomed them" (Rom 14:2–3). In other words, people's moral convictions are none of our business. Instead of always judging different viewpoints as "I'm right and you're wrong," we should say, "I see it from this perspective, and you see it from that perspective. Let's learn from each other."

Once, a man wrote to an acquaintance who was facing a difficult situation. He said, "Please know that whatever you say, whatever you do, I will never judge you. I will know that there is a good reason for your behavior. I believe in you. I accept you!" Jesus did not have a credal or religious bias.

Now, if this were today, Jesus would still accept all people just as they are! In turn, this would enable them to become *more* than they are. When Mother Teresa first arrived in Calcutta and tried to establish a hospice for the homeless, the nun and her fellow sisters faced neighborhood hostility. None of the citizens wanted the church's "home for the dying" in their backyard. And because her mission was located near a Hindu temple, its holy men also objected. But when one of the Hindu priests was diagnosed with terminal tuberculosis, because the city hospital admitted only people who could be cured, he was denied a bed. Mother Teresa welcomed him to her hospice and graciously cared for him until he died. Then she delivered his body to the temple for Hindu rites. News of her ecumenical compassion spread throughout the city, and the rest, as they say, is history.

If Jesus were here today, would he still interact with all people, even those who are socially unacceptable? Would he converse with Muslims and Buddhists? Would he drink coffee with a prostitute? Even though some standards would be different if Jesus lived in America today, his basic responses concerning different genders, races, and religions would remain the same.

Chapter 5

Jesus Uses a Child's Lunch

In a cartoon a little boy is holding some coins and talking to two disciples. He says, "Yeah! Normally I do carry five barley loaves and two small fish, but today my mom gave me money to buy a hot lunch."

The story about Jesus using a child's lunch to feed five thousand people is well known: One evening, after a long day of teaching and healing, the crowds didn't want to leave. Jesus tried to get away to eat and rest, but "he saw a great crowd; and he had compassion for them, because they were like sheep without a shepherd; and he began to teach them many things" (Mark 6:34). John adds the detail about the source of the food; it was a little child who shared his lunch. Andrew said to Jesus, "There is a boy here who has five barley loaves and two fish. But what are they among so many people?" (John 6:9).

Jesus always felt compassion for needy people, and he always did something about it. When Jesus refused to dismiss the crowd, the disciples were aggravated, but Jesus couldn't turn away hurting people. He was determined to fill the need. He began by taking inventory of their resources. After doing so, he began to organize the chaotic situation. Then Jesus prayed and began to feed the people.

Jesus always responded to legitimate problems with practical solutions. He did this because he loved people.

We are called not only to love, but to show that love. Service is the concrete method we use to do that. Lack of spiritual maturity and human kindness are the greatest deterrents to others accepting Christ. Our greatest service is to be good examples of concern and responsibility.

Why do you suppose Jesus responded to this event as he did? What lessons can we learn from this incident? What point does he make about charity? First, Jesus had empathy for human needs. He didn't go around handing out meals on a regular basis, but in this case, through no fault of their own, the people were hungry. It wasn't because of laziness or poor money management. It was because they had stayed and listened to Jesus in an isolated place until it was too late to go home or into town for food. This was a legitimate human need.

If Jesus were here today, he would still have empathy for others. Over and over, the scriptures say he had compassion for the people. He felt the pain of all the oppressed, confused, and ill men and women who came to him for help. Once, when Bishop Desmond Tutu, winner of the 1984 Nobel Peace Prize, was asked by one of the other bishops what we could do in the world to promote peace, he gazed into the distance for a moment, then answered in a quiet voice, "You must care." That was Jesus's trademark: He cared. Jesus noticed problems and tried to help people.

Next, Jesus used what was available. It's significant that he didn't even consider turning stones into bread. He didn't pray for manna to come down from heaven. We never see him waving magic wands to produce miracles. Instead, he allowed the people to be part of the solution. That's the important point of this story: A child shared, and the disciples served. The Bible never promises something from nothing.

If Jesus were here today, he would still use available resources. He refused to turn stones into bread during his temptation, and he never did such things during his ministry. On another occasion, when his own disciples were hungry on the sabbath, he didn't create miraculous manna. He allowed them simply to pick the wheat (see Matt 12:1).

Today, we should use what we have. There are many agricultural opportunities in America. No one should be hungry. Jesus would use all the resources available to help people.

Finally, Jesus avoided waste. After the people ate, the scriptures say, "They took up twelve baskets full of broken pieces and of the fish" (Mark 6:43). Some people have an "easy come/easy go" mentality; but that's not good stewardship. One of the worst consequences of a wealthy society is the idea that small things don't matter. As Americans we throw out more than many nations possess. Each of us has a limited amount of time, energy, and physical resources. We must use them well. Jesus conserved the scraps; the disciples picked up the broken pieces.

Even in the story of the prodigal son, Jesus indicated that wasting his money was one of the young man's most regrettable sins (see Luke 15:13). Solomon said, "Anyone who tills the land will have plenty of bread, but one who follows worthless pursuits will have plenty of poverty" (Prov 28:19).

If Jesus were here today, he would still be sensible and frugal. He wouldn't waste money or food. He instructed his disciples to carefully gather up the leftovers. We don't know if they used them or sent them home with the people, but they were certainly not left to rot.

In a nation of plenty, frugality is often neglected and even ridiculed, but Jesus was frugal. He owned few possessions. He summed up his lifestyle when some men wanted to follow him by saying, "Foxes have holes, and birds of the air have nests; but the Son of Man has nowhere to lay his head" (Matt 8:20). We should be careful with our resources. People should learn how to make do and stretch their food dollars. Jesus was frugal and practical in the use of his assets.

Now, if this were today, Jesus would still try to meet people's needs. He was realistic and pragmatic. His brother James probably reflected Jesus's philosophy when he wrote, "If a brother or sister is naked and lacks daily food, and one of you says to them, 'Go in peace; keep warm and eat your fill,' and yet you do not supply their bodily needs, what is the good of that?" (Jas 2:15–16).

One man wrote, "I was hungry, and you organized a charity to discuss my hunger. I was imprisoned, and you crept quietly to your chapel and prayed for my release. I was naked, and you debated the morality of my appearance. I was sick, and you thanked God for your health. I was homeless, and you preached to me about the spiritual shelter of God's love. I was lonely, and you left me by myself and went to church. You seem so holy, so close to God. But I'm still very hungry and cold and lonely. What does it profit a man to repeat his prayers and sing his hymns when the rest of the world is crying for help?" We must care, and we must share, but we must not do it in a way that shames people or encourages them to remain helpless. Benevolence is harmful unless it respects the recipients and enables them to become more independent.

A successful businessman in New York City stood on a street corner every winter and gave away gloves. When someone asked him why he did that, he explained, "There was a time, many years ago, when I was very poor and could not afford to buy a pair. I remember how cold my hands got and how much I envied people who had gloves." Most of us forget; this man remembered.

Our needs should make us sensitive to others who have those needs. A person who has known hunger can identify with a person who has gone without food. A former prisoner knows what it feels like for another person to lose his freedom. Someone who has been very ill understands how lonely and depressing it is to be hospitalized or shut in.

If he were here today, would Jesus run a permanent soup kitchen? Would he throw a big cookout for the homeless? Would he vote for more food stamps? Well, it's a different world now. Food is more readily available. There are also many agencies set up to feed the hungry both here and abroad.

We don't know for sure what Jesus would do if he lived in America today, but we do know that he would still care. He would still use whatever resources are available to fill people's needs, and he would not waste anything in the process.

Chapter 6

Jesus Defends a Fallen Woman

A motivational speaker who was energizing a group of salesmen said, "Now, fellows, when it comes to sincerity, there's only one rule, 'Always be sincere, whether you mean it or not.'"

Well, it makes a big difference to God whether we mean it or not. The psalmist said, "You desire truth in the inward being" (Ps 51:6). Paul said, "If I speak in the tongues of mortals and of angels, but do not have love, I am a noisy gong or a clanging cymbal" (1 Cor 13:1). John said, "Those who say, 'I love God,' and hate their brothers or sisters, are liars" (1 John 4:20). All of these scriptures involve being genuine and honest and sincere.

A wonderful incident in Jesus's life showed a sinful woman's sincerity:

> One of the Pharisees asked Jesus to eat with him, and he went into the Pharisee's house and took his place at the table. And a woman in the city, who was a sinner, having learned that he was eating in the Pharisee's house, brought an alabaster jar of ointment. She stood behind him at his feet, weeping, and began to bathe his feet with her tears and to dry them with her

hair. Then she continued kissing his feet and anointing them with the ointment. (Luke 7:36–38)

This was a most unusual and daring act for a woman, even more so since she was a prostitute. It got a lot of attention and, of course, the inevitable criticism: "Now when the Pharisee who had invited him saw it, he said to himself, 'If this man were a prophet, he would have known who and what kind of woman this is who is touching him—that she is a sinner'" (Luke 7:39).

We don't know if Simon said this out loud or if he whispered it to a companion. Either Jesus or one of his disciples overheard, and Jesus responded, "'Do you see this woman? I entered your house; you gave me no water for my feet, but she has bathed my feet with her tears and dried them with her hair. You gave me no kiss, but from the time I came in she has not stopped kissing my feet. You did not anoint my head with oil, but she anointed my feet with ointment. Therefore, I tell you, her sins, which were many, have been forgiven; hence she has shown great love'" (see Luke 7:44–47).

The room was probably deathly silent when Jesus finished speaking, but he was mainly concerned about the woman's feelings. He turned to her and announced clearly for everyone to hear, "Your sins are forgiven" (Luke 7:48).

Matthew may be relating another version of this event when he describes a woman who demonstrated her affection. Again, there was criticism—this time from Jesus's own disciples. Jesus replied, "Why do you trouble the woman? She has performed a good service for me. For you always have the poor with you, but you will not always have me. By pouring this ointment on my body she has prepared me for burial. Truly I tell you, wherever this good news is proclaimed in the whole world, what she has done will be told in remembrance of her" (see Matt 26:10–13). Again, Jesus defended the woman for her love and compassion. He wasn't as interested in the specific actions as he was with her motive.

Why do you suppose Jesus responded the way he did in these situations? What lessons can we learn from them? What point do they make about sincerity? First, the woman felt deep concern. She was willing to violate custom and put herself at risk for condemnation and maybe even punishment. She crashed a party. She touched a male. She associated with people out of her social class. She didn't let public opinion influence her decision.

If Jesus were here today, he would still appreciate honest concern. He realized that this woman didn't give in order to receive a reward. She didn't give in order to hear praise. She really cared. Jesus said, "She has shown great love" (Luke 7:47). To Jesus, love was proof of dedication.

Sincerity is essential. There is an old story about a man who dreamed that he was in church one Sunday morning. He saw the musician playing and the praise team singing, but he heard no sound. The congregation was singing, but the sound was muted. When the minister rose to speak, his lips moved, but there was no volume. The man asked the Lord for an explanation, and a voice said, "That's how this service sounds in heaven. You hear nothing because there is nothing to hear. The people are engaged in a form of worship, but their thoughts are on other things, and their hearts are far away!" Jesus blesses people who feel concern for others.

Next, the woman showed real feelings. She was tearful as she ministered and served. She wasn't ashamed to show emotions. There was no mask or false front. There was no pretense. She wasn't flattering Jesus or trying to impress him. She was simply expressing her affection and gratitude.

In today's world, emotions are often hidden, but Jesus always showed his feelings. The scripture says, "As he came near and saw the city, he wept over it" (Luke 19:41). He also wept at Lazarus's tomb (see John 11:35). Deceit is deadly. The psalmist said, "No one who practices deceit shall remain in my house; no one who utters lies shall continue in my presence" (Ps 101:7).

If Jesus were here today, he would still appreciate real feelings. He detested hypocrisy. He recognized and appreciated this woman's empathetic nature. The scriptures refer to genuine emotions as coming from a pure heart: "Those who have clean hands and pure hearts…will receive blessing from the LORD" (Ps 24:4–5). Later, the writer of Hebrews expressed it this way: "Let us approach with a true heart in full assurance of faith" (Heb 10:22). Jesus blessed people who are honest and willing to share their real feelings.

Finally, the woman used her resources. This woman was not wealthy. She probably spent her entire dowry on this one grand gesture of appreciation and worship. It wasn't a practical thing to do. In fact, it's probably not something Jesus would have advised her to do. However, he realized her pure motives and accepted the tribute graciously.

If Jesus were here today, he would still appreciate generous acts. But he would also point out that why we do something is often more important than what we do. He was not necessarily commending the woman for the actual gift of perfume. Rather, he was commending her for the love and generosity that prompted the gift. She showed her love for Jesus when so few did. Her attitude was similar to that of the poor widow whom Jesus praised (see Luke 21:2–4). Jesus blessed and rewarded people for actions that reveal sincere dedication.

According to legend, an angel who was observing people's behavior noticed a hungry newsboy who had fallen asleep. A couple came by, and the woman quietly put a dollar into his pocket and was walking away when the young man with her went back and gave another dollar. An old lady standing by gave him a quarter, and another man handed over a small coin. All in all, the little boy received almost three dollars.

Delighted, the angel returned to notify the divine recordkeeper about the good deeds. "I know," said the recording angel. "It's all written down!" But the book showed only a dollar and a quarter. The recordkeeper explained, "You see, that young girl gave a dollar out of love, and the old lady gave a quarter out of pity, but the young man only gave because he wanted to impress his date, and the other man gave because he didn't want to be considered stingy. Those last two don't count."

Now, if this were today, would Jesus still consider people's motives for service? Would Jesus accept some personal gift from a Las Vegas showgirl? Would he allow such intimate personal attention from a well-known prostitute? Would he accept a strange and excessive gesture of admiration from a questionable character?

We don't know exactly what Jesus would do if something like this happened in America today, but we do know he would still be appreciative and gracious.

Chapter 7

Jesus Enables a Traitor to Change

An old mountaineer in a large city for the first time stood near an elevator. He watched as an old, wrinkled woman hobbled in and the doors closed. In a few minutes the doors opened, and a young, attractive woman walked out. Suddenly, realizing the possibilities, he yelled to his son, "Hey, boy! Hurry up! Go get your mama!"

All of us wish change were that easy. But it's not. The Bible tells the story of a man who made a drastic change in both his priorities and his lifestyle. Zacchaeus was a shrewd and capable person. To be a chief of the tax collectors was a prestigious position that provided a person with authority, influence, and the opportunity to acquire great wealth. Nevertheless, Zacchaeus was obviously unhappy and unfulfilled. He was different from the rich fool who planned to eat, drink, and be merry. He had deeper desires. Material possessions didn't satisfy him. Zacchaeus had probably heard rumors about Jesus and really wanted to meet him. In fact, he was desperate, but he had a problem: "He was short in stature" (Luke 19:3).

This was a man who solved problems. He was determined and resourceful—the same traits that had made him a successful government official. He climbed a tree so he could see as Jesus passed by, and Jesus picked Zacchaeus out of the crowd, rewarding him for his initiative: "Zacchaeus, hurry and come down; for I must stay at your house today" (see Luke 19:5).

That was an astonishing statement. Most Jews hated tax collectors. They were considered the lowest of traitors. They were also viewed as thieves because all the extra money they squeezed out of the people went into their own pockets. Zacchaeus was certainly surprised, but he didn't hesitate for a moment.

Of course, there are always critics, and this incident was no exception. But Jesus knew Zacchaeus wasn't just professing with his lips. He was ready to put his money where his mouth was. Jesus didn't demand or even suggest that he must change his attitude or lifestyle. Instead, Zacchaeus realized what he needed to do: "Zacchaeus stood there and said to the Lord, 'Look, half of my possessions, Lord, I will give to the poor; and if I have defrauded anyone of anything, I will pay back four times as much'" (Luke 19:8). This generous commitment represented a drastic change in priorities, and Jesus validated his decision, saying, "Today salvation has come to this house" (Luke 19:9).

That sycamore tree has become the site of one of the greatest salvation experiences in the history of Christianity. This incident shows the power of kindness in effecting change. Suppose Jesus had paused under that tree, looked up at Zacchaeus, and called out to him, "You child of the devil! You sinner, who cheats the poor and turns orphans and widows out on the streets, how shall you escape the damnation of hell?" If Jesus had denounced him in this way, it's almost certain we never would have heard of Zacchaeus. Indeed, if that's the way Jesus had responded to people, we probably never would have heard of him either. Instead, Jesus spoke kindly to him and went to his house as a guest. He did all of this before Zacchaeus had made any apologies, commitments, or promises to change.

Why do you suppose Jesus reacted as he did to Zacchaeus? What lessons can we learn from this incident? What point does it make about change? First, Jesus responded to Zacchaeus because Zacchaeus really wanted to change. There were a lot of eager men and women on the street that day, but Jesus responded to Zacchaeus because he realized he was a serious seeker. Mere curiosity is not enough. Many people are attracted to some new doctrine, but they aren't serious enough to make a commitment. Zacchaeus may have heard about Jesus and how he accepted and forgave sinners. He may have yearned for that acceptance and forgiveness.

If Jesus were here today, he would still respond to those who want to change. He always issued an invitation and left it up to individuals to take the initiative: "Let anyone who is thirsty come to me, and let the one who believes in me drink'" (John 7:37–38). Notice he said *anyone*, not just good, moral Americans.

Jesus said, "Come to me, all you that are weary and are carrying heavy burdens, and I will give you rest" (Matt 11:28). Notice he said *all*, not just those who are socially acceptable. Such a welcoming attitude is much more likely to lead to a conversion than a condemning attitude. In the old fable of the wind and the sun, a debate ensued as to which could make a man take off his cloak. The wind tried. It stormed and raged and blew, but the man only wrapped his cloak tighter about him. When the wind gave up, the sun shined warmly upon the man until, heated by its rays, he willingly removed his garment. We can learn from the methods of the sun. We can also learn from Jesus's response that day when he dealt kindly with an outcast publican and brought out the best in him. Jesus always accepts those who are willing to change.

Next, Jesus responded to Zacchaeus because he was determined to change. Jesus reached out to Zacchaeus because he saw his resolve and ingenuity. Just a vague wish for a better life is not enough. Change requires determination. Zacchaeus didn't make excuses and say, "Well, I can't see him, so why try?" He didn't let others stand in his way. He didn't shrug and say, "Oh well, he'll probably come by here again, and I'll see him then." Instead, he showed initiative and persistence. He risked criticism and ridicule. This professional man ran down the street and actually climbed a tree. If Jesus were here today, he would still respond to those who show determination to change.

Furthermore, Jesus always rewarded persistence. The men who were so desperate to help a sick friend that they tore off the roof were rewarded (see Mark 2:3–5). Also, a Syro-Phoenician woman who argued with him was rewarded. It was almost unheard of for a woman to be so outspoken with a man. Instead of reproach, Jesus complimented her (Matt 15:26–28).

Zacchaeus was willing to climb a tree. The four men were willing to remove a roof. The Syro-Phoenician woman was willing to argue her case. In each of these incidences Jesus equated persistence with faith. Jesus blesses those who are determined to change.

Finally, Jesus responded to Zacchaeus because he did what was necessary to change. He didn't just *hope* for a better life. He didn't just *think* about his values. He didn't just *talk* about improvement. He actually did something! Jesus offered complete forgiveness because Zacchaeus put feet to his prayers. He was ready to do something about his situation, even if it meant personal and financial sacrifice. He didn't just *repent*; he *atoned*. He made amends. He changed both his mind and his actions. He volunteered to give half of his fortune away and to repay those he had cheated fourfold.

Few people are willing to make such a drastic change in their lifestyle. If Jesus were here today, he would still respond to those who are willing to do what is necessary to change. He believed trees were to be evaluated by their fruits (see Matt 7:17). He also said, "Not everyone who says to me, 'Lord, Lord,' will enter the kingdom of heaven, but only the one who does the will of my Father in heaven" (Matt 7:21). James agreed: "So faith by itself, if it has no works, is dead. But someone will say, 'You have faith and I have works. Show me your faith apart from your works, and I by my works will show you my faith" (Jas 2:17–18). Zacchaeus followed through. He demonstrated his sincerity by his actions. Jesus blesses those who are willing to do whatever is necessary to change.

There's a little bug that crawls around in a stagnant pond. It enjoys the mud on the bottom of the swamp and ignores the green scum on the top. It is unmindful of the sunshine above. One day, this little creature becomes restless with an urgent desire to climb to the surface. It wants a better life. Laboriously, it makes its way up the stalk of some reed until it reaches fresh air. It is determined to change. Suddenly, its shell bursts open and releases a beautiful creature known as the dragonfly. It is willing to give up its old skin and its old habitat to change. Now, it despises the mud and the dark scum of the stagnant pond. It lives on a higher plane and enjoys the beauties of God's creation. That's what happened to Zacchaeus.

What if this were today? How would Jesus react if some unpopular skinflint climbed up a light pole to get his attention? Would Jesus go home with a criminal? Would Jesus socialize with a known drug dealer? Would Jesus publicly validate a person who had stolen thousands of dollars from innocent people? Would Jesus buck public opinion by associating with a traitor?

We don't know for sure what would happen if a parallel event occurred on a street in our town. Even though many details would be different if Jesus lived in American today, his willingness to help us change our lives would remain the same.

Chapter 8

Jesus Confronts a Vengeful Mob

Once, a devoted mother received a picture of her soldier son marching with his company. "Why, look!" she exclaimed to her friend. "Every one of those men is out of step except my Johnny." That's a typical reaction. We think everybody is wrong except us.

Blaming others for their faults and mistakes while ignoring our own shortcomings is human nature, but it leads to hypocrisy. When religious leaders brought before Jesus a woman caught in the act of adultery, they were looking for someone to condemn, and they were trying to trap Jesus according to his response (see John 8:1–6).

It's significant that they didn't bring the man involved. We don't know if he ran away or if he became part of the hostile, accusing crowd. But we do know they wanted to humiliate the poor woman. Of course, they justified their cruelty by quoting Scripture. Many self-righteous do-gooders use Scripture to judge everyone except themselves.

As usual, the accusers' purpose was not to improve morals. Their motive was not to make life better. They were really trying to ensnare Jesus with a theological question. However, Jesus didn't argue or debate the question. He avoided the trap and returned the problem to the accusers, essentially saying, "Sure! Follow the commandment to the letter, but there's one requirement: You can only do that if you are able to prove that you are sinless and therefore qualified to be the judge, jury, and executioner."

Suddenly, the accusers lost their arrogance. Every member of that crowd knew they had broken the laws and committed sins. Such self-examination is very unpleasant. These eager critics obviously did not want to analyze or discuss their own personal situations. They quickly decided to duck the issue (see John 8:9).

We don't know what the victim was thinking or expecting, but she didn't run away.

She chose to stand near the only person who had ever shown her tolerance and forgiveness. After the hypocritical judges backed down and left, Jesus and the woman were alone. He treated her with kindness: "Woman, where are they? Has no one condemned you?' She said, 'No one, sir.' and Jesus said, 'Neither do I'" (John 8:10–11).

It's so easy to throw stones. It's so easy to see our friends' flaws. It's so easy to point out other people's problems. It's so easy to place blame. It's so easy to censure, reproach, and accuse. It's so easy to see a smudge on our neighbor's face while we overlook the ugly sneer on our own face. It's the Pharisee mentality all over again. Judgment is one of the most common human failings. Someone said, "Constructive criticism is when I criticize you! Destructive criticism is when you criticize me!"

Why do you suppose Jesus treated this woman as he did? What lessons can we learn from this incident? What point does it make about hypocrisy? First, hypocrites always have ulterior motives. It pays to take criticism with a grain of salt. These people didn't care about that woman's soul. They didn't care about the morals of their community. They didn't care about solving a social problem. They had a hidden motive. They wanted to trap Jesus, and they didn't hesitate to use this poor woman as a pawn in their scheme. Both Jesus and Paul warned against such judgment (see Luke 6:37; Rom 2:1).

If Jesus were here today, he would still recognize such hypocrisy. Things aren't always as they appear on the surface. Those who are outwardly moral may be inwardly immoral. Few people judge and criticize others out of honest concern! Most of us point fingers to distract attention from our own flaws and justify our own mistakes. Jesus would oppose moralists who have ulterior motives.

Next, hypocrites are always critical of others. Since we are all sinners, it's impossible for us to be impartial and objective. As human beings we have blind spots. We have personal prejudices. We have human weaknesses. We have hidden shadows. We tend to evaluate sins by our own standards. In short, most of us believe the things we do are reasonable and excusable but the things others do must be denounced and condemned. However, we must get rid of our own problems before we can understand others.

If Jesus were here today, he would still confront the judges. In fact, the hypocritical religious leaders and the self-righteous Pharisees were the only individuals Jesus ever really accused. He stood up to these particular individuals because their habits are destructive to families, communities, and churches. Jesus's story about the tares emphasizes the danger of trying to rid the world of evil (see Matt 13:27–30). Furthermore, as long as people are judging others and pulling weeds, they are not having to deal with their own shortcomings. Jesus would oppose moralists who constantly criticize others.

Finally, hypocrites are always eager to avoid blame. People who are mature enough to be qualified to judge fairly don't want to judge. Truly righteous people don't need to distract from their own sins by pointing fingers at others. Instead, it's fearful, bitter, and miserable people who are constantly looking for flaws in their associates. Insecure individuals criticize others to make themselves look better, but it doesn't work. They are merely revealing their own problems. Our judgment about others says more about our own weaknesses and faults than it does about the other person's weaknesses and faults. Jesus would agree with the wise person who said, "Reformers try to fix others. Saints fix themselves."

If Jesus were here today, he would still avoid judging. Jesus knew attacks are never productive. People can't be threatened into the kingdom, frightened into the kingdom, or shamed into the kingdom. Jesus summarized his entire life mission this way: "I do not judge anyone who hears my words and does not keep them, for I came not to judge the world, but to save the world" (John 12:47). If Jesus did not believe it was his purpose to judge, why do we think it's ours? Jesus would oppose moralists who are eager to avoid blame.

Once, at a spiritual retreat, the participants were asked to find a smooth rock and personalize it. On one side they were to paint their own name; on the other side they were to write, "Let anyone among you who is without sin be the first to throw a stone at her" (see John 8:7). One woman said, "In all the years I've carried that stone, I've touched it; I've clenched my angry fist around it. But I have never been able to cast it! God knows I've tried. I've wanted to throw a big rock at someone else's mistake. I've wanted to hurl a crushing boulder at someone who has hurt me. But when I reach for that 'first stone,' something makes me realize I don't meet the requirements for judging and punishing another person."

If this were today, what sinner would the "moralists" bring to Jesus? Would it be an alcoholic? Would it be a porn star? Would it be a drug addict? We don't know who they would choose, but we know it wouldn't be out of honest concern. Even though Jesus's accusers would be different if he lived in America today, his basic responses concerning judging fairly and respecting others would still be the same.

Chapter 9

Jesus Deals with Ambitious Disciples

At a T-ball game, a little boy came up to bat. He swatted the ball off the tee and ran as fast as he could to third base. The coach said, "Son, you sure hit that ball a long way, but why did you run to third base instead of to first?" The little boy replied, "Well, that was the fastest way to get where I wanted to go."

That's a common problem. We want to get there faster, so we skip steps on the way to success. Two of Jesus's disciples were like that. They were overly ambitious. They wanted honor, power, and important positions. Furthermore, they wanted them without putting forth any effort. The scriptures say, "James and John…came forward to him and said to him, 'Teacher, we want you to do for us whatever we ask of you.' And he said to them, 'What is it you want me to do for you?' And they said to him, 'Grant us to sit, one at your right hand and one at your left, in your glory'" (Mark 10:35–37).

Now, this wasn't just a request about seating arrangements. In that day, those who sat on the right and left of a ruler were second in command, like vice presidents or secretaries of state. This was a request about authority and prestige. In fact, sitting on the right hand of God was the figurative position that Jesus himself would occupy (see Acts 5:31).

Jesus's reply was discouraging: "'You do not know what you are asking.... To sit at my right hand or at my left is not mine to grant, but it is for those for whom it has been prepared'" (Mark 10:38, 40).

Matthew gives another version of this incident: "Then the mother of the sons of Zebedee came to him with her sons, and kneeling before him, she asked a favor of him. And he said to her, 'What do you want?' She said to him, 'Declare that these two sons of mine will sit, one at your right hand and one at your left, in your kingdom'" (Matt 20:20–21).

This intercession by the mother of James and John indicates that ambition was probably a family trait. Again, Jesus explains that success can't be given. When the other disciples heard about this incident, they were jealous, at which point Jesus stopped everything and taught them a lesson: "You know that among the Gentiles those whom they recognize as their rulers lord it over them, and their great ones are tyrants over them. But it is not so among you; but whoever wishes to become great among you must be your servant, and whoever wishes to be first among you must be slave of all" (Mark 10:42–44).

Many people want to skip steps. They want the success, the rewards, and the status of a high position without working for it. That doesn't just happen! Once, when an author became well known, a cynical woman said, "No one had ever heard of that man a year ago. He just woke up one morning and found himself famous."

"Madam," the author's friend replied, "on the morning that man woke up and 'found himself famous,' he had been writing eight hours a day for fifteen years."

The ignorant and the indolent see only the effects of things, not the causes. They talk of luck and chance because they don't understand the process.

Why do you suppose Jesus responded to James and John as he did? What lessons can we learn from this incident? What point was he making about ambition? First, Jesus indicated that ambition is okay. He didn't condemn James and John for aspiring to a high position. Even Jesus had considered taking shortcuts to success. Two of his temptations involved this issue. Jumping off the temple would have given him instant notoriety and credibility. Worshiping Satan would have resulted in a quick rise to worldly power. But he rejected both.

Almost everyone wants to be somebody, but few are determined enough to do what it takes to reach their goal. Paul admitted having ambition, but he also condemned selfish ambition (see Rom 15:20; Phil. 2:3). If Jesus were here today, he would emphasize the fact that there are many levels of service that cannot be achieved without ambition. We need to have personal desires and personal goals and personal dreams. Jesus would encourage unselfish and productive ambitions.

Next, Jesus explained that success must be earned. A parent can't give a child maturity. A teacher can't give a student an education. A businessman can't give an employee success. These things must be earned. Abraham Lincoln said, "No matter how tall your grandfather was, you have to do your own growing."

When young people get too much too soon, they never mature. Many famous men's sons and daughters are unproductive. A butterfly that's helped out of its cocoon can never fly. The struggle for freedom is an essential element. Earning something gives dignity, worth, and confidence. If Jesus were here today, he would emphasize that success must be earned. Those who rush through their period of preparation live to regret it. In order to be your best, you must have discipline. You must be willing to dedicate your energy, your time, and your efforts to change your ambition into a positive reality.

When a heavyweight champion of the world won an Olympic gold medal, many young boys dreamed of becoming boxers. One teenager decided to hire a private trainer. The teacher told him the required course consisted of twenty lessons. The student agreed and had his first lesson. After a tough, painful sparring session, the battered youth had some questions: "Did you say there are twenty lessons in this course, and I just took one today? And I have to finish all of them before I can earn any money boxing?"

"That's right," answered the teacher.

After a moment the student asked, "Well, sir, I wonder if I could take the other nineteen lessons by correspondence?"

Unfortunately, you can't take life's lessons by correspondence. You must experience them! Jesus would encourage those who are willing to work to achieve their ambitions.

Finally, Jesus emphasized that teamwork is productive. Some people seem to believe that the only way they can be up is to put you down. This seesaw mentality is immature and unproductive. Such wrangling over status is useless. It also destroys the unity and morale of any group or organization. That's wrong! If Jesus were here today, he would still emphasize mutual support.

We must not have an atmosphere of jealousy and envy in spiritual circles. Instead, we need cooperation and support. Envy is a shameful flaw. It destroys the joy of every accomplishment. It makes an enemy out of every opponent. Jesus would encourage those who cooperate with others to reach their goal.

If this were today, we know Jesus would want us to take personal responsibility in the areas of growth and success. He would never advocate easy shortcuts or indicate that we can have success without effort. He would never want us to reach our goals by destroying others.

A party of businessmen who went hunting each year always hired the same guide. One year, however, that guide wasn't available, so they hired a substitute. He explained to the hunters that he knew a shorter way. Against their better judgment, they followed and soon became hopelessly lost. Later, they had to be rescued by the experienced guide. "I guess we learned the hard lesson," observed one of the hunters. "When a man has a map and a guide, he'd better leave the shortcuts alone!"

We have a map and a guide. We have the Bible, and we have Jesus's example. We must avoid shortcuts.

If Jesus were here today, would he condemn young people with lofty goals? Of course not! Would he discourage people from seeking promotions? No! Would he criticize those with high aspirations? He wouldn't do that because he knows our success honors God.

We don't know exactly what Jesus would do if he lived in America today, but we do know his basic responses about earning our promotions and avoiding shortcuts would still be the same.

Chapter 10

Jesus Emphasizes Forgiveness

An angry lady pushed her shopping cart through the express lane at the supermarket. Before the clerk said a word, she yelled, "Listen, Buster, I work two jobs. I got shafted in a divorce! My car's making a weird noise. My kid dyed her hair pink, and my dog just had thirteen pups! So don't tell me I have one item too many unless you have a death wish!"

This depicts the fragile state of many people's nerves today. Most of us live on the edge. That's why there's so much conflict and violence in our world. Jesus was concerned about social relationships. He emphasized patience, tolerance, and forgiveness. One of his most dramatic stories deals with this issue. Peter instigated the discussion when he asked about forgiveness (see Matt 18:21).

Peter probably thought Jesus would be pleased with his question. The rabbis taught an obligation to forgive three times. Peter suggested seven. In Jewish law, seven represented completeness. Forgiving seven times seemed to represent the ultimate in generosity, but Jesus never advocated such legalism. He replied, "Not seven times, I tell you, seventy-seven times" (Matt 18:22).

Since keeping count of enumerable events would be impossible, Jesus insinuates that we should maintain a constant attitude of forgiveness. To further illustrate this important concept, he told an unforgettable story:

> The kingdom of heaven may be compared to a king who wished to settle accounts with his slaves. When he began the reckoning, one who owed him ten thousand talents was brought to him; and, as he could not pay, his lord ordered him to be sold, together with his wife and children and all his possessions, and payment to be made. So the slave fell on his knees before him, saying, "Have patience with me, and I will pay you everything." And out of pity for him, the lord of that slave released him and forgave him the debt. (Matt 18:23–27)

Notice that the master didn't do merely what the servant asked; he did much more. Instead of giving him a longer time to pay, he canceled the entire debt. That should have made the servant happy and grateful, but it didn't! His attitude and the actions that followed are unbelievably selfish and cruel. Jesus continued, "But that same slave, as he went out, came upon one of his fellow slaves who owed him a hundred denarii; and seizing him by the throat, he said, 'Pay what you owe.' Then his fellow slave fell down and pleaded with him, 'Have patience with me, and I will pay you.' But he refused; then he went and threw him into prison until he would pay the debt" (Matt 18:28–30).

This reaction was so unfair that bystanders reported the matter to the master. The generous master was furious and took immediate action. He reprimanded the servant, saying, "'You wicked slave! I forgave you all that debt because you pleaded with me. Should you not have had mercy on your fellow slave, as I had mercy on you?' And in anger his lord handed him over to be tortured until he would pay his entire debt" (Matt 18:32–34).

The first amount was probably almost a million dollars, and the other only ten or twelve dollars. Jesus used this great discrepancy to show how trivial most of our little aggravations appear when compared to God's total and complete forgiveness of all our sins.

Why do you suppose Jesus used such a striking analogy to illustrate this concept? What lessons can we learn from this parable? What point is he making about forgiveness? First, Jesus emphasized that God forgives us. The old ideas about an angry, vindictive deity were wrong. Jesus revealed God as a loving and merciful Father. He indicated that God does more than we expect and gives us more than we ask for. This generous benefactor canceled the entire amount and set him free. That's what God does.

If Jesus were here today, he would still describe a God of love. That's important, because we tend to become like the God we worship. If we believe in a wrathful God, full of hatred and intolerance, we'll feel justified in holding on to our own hostility and resentment. The "eye for an eye" motto is causing violence all over the world. God doesn't hold grudges and mete out arbitrary punishment. He cancels our debt and wipes the slate clean. Jesus would assure us that God loves and forgives us.

Next, Jesus emphasized that we must accept God's forgiveness. Mistakes are inevitable. We can't go through life without making selfish decisions and doing hurtful things. No one is perfect! Paul said, "There is no one who is righteous, not even one" (Rom 3:10). James went further: "Whoever keeps the whole law but fails in one point has become accountable for all of it" (Jas 2:10).

Trying to deny and cover our own sins keeps us from growing. It makes us judgmental and critical. If Jesus were here today, he would still emphasize our need for forgiveness. He would try to eradicate bigotry and hypocrisy. He would probably recommend much of the material in the twelve-step program of Alcoholics Anonymous. It requires members to make a searching inventory of themselves, admit to God and others the exact nature of their wrong attitudes and activities, be ready to have God remove their character defects, ask God to remove their shortcomings, make a list of everyone they have harmed, and make amends whenever possible.

Jesus would insist that we recognize and admit our own part in disagreements and conflicts. It's obvious that when we see our own faults, we'll be much more tolerant of our friends' faults. Jesus would urge us to admit our mistakes and confess our faults.

Finally, Jesus emphasized that we must forgive others. It's wrong to judge, criticize, and resent our friends or associates. We can never realize our own forgiveness and freedom unless we extend it to others. In fact, if you hold hatred in your heart, then you cannot accept God's forgiveness! If Jesus were here today, he'd still say, "Be merciful, just as your Father is merciful" (Luke 6:36). Jesus even indicated that forgiveness must be extended before we can pray and worship.

Just four months after one woman became a Christian, she faced an agonizing test of her faith. Her daughter was stabbed to death. Despite overwhelming grief, she held fast to her belief in humanity's goodness and opposed the "death penalty." This woman believed in separating the sin from the sinner. She said, "It diminishes all of us to frame an individual by a single act." If somebody kills a person, they are labeled as a *murderer*. Afterward, that becomes their definition. That's all people focus on. This label blocks off everything else about that person. Obviously, that may be one true fact about them, but it isn't the sum total. People are more than their sin. Jesus would make forgiveness a major theme of his teachings and offer second chances.

If this were today, we know Jesus would still encourage us to offer forgiveness. We must discover and defuse our anger. Rage hurts immediately, and resentments hurt over the long term. Jesus would probably counsel individuals concerning domestic abuse and hold anger-management seminars. Jesus practiced forgiveness. Even when he was dying on the cross, he said, "Father, forgive them; for they do not know what they are doing" (Luke 23:34).

If Jesus were telling a modern story, would he talk about bitter individuals who hold grudges? Would he rebuke those who say, "I don't get mad; I get even"? Would he denounce "road rage"? Would he expect husbands and wives and families, fragmented by divorce, to have forgiving attitudes? How would he handle crimes and court cases and the death penalty? Would he apply this principle of forgiveness to nations involved in conflicts and wars?

We don't know what examples he would use, but even though the specific details of his stories would be different if he lived in America today, his basic teachings about forgiveness would still be the same.

Chapter 11

Jesus Commands Tolerance and Concern

After reading about the good Samaritan, the Sunday school teacher asked, "Now, what does that story teach us?" One little girl quickly raised her hand and said, "It teaches us that if I'm in trouble, you're supposed to help me!"

Most of us would agree with her. We're very self-centered. We think of everything from our own viewpoint. We evaluate everything by asking, "How will this affect me?" Furthermore, our survival instinct causes us to consider those who are not like us as our enemies. That's an innate tendency, but we must get beyond our own concerns. We must also look out for the concerns of others. We're becoming a very small planet. With new communication channels and new transportation methods, anything that happens to one person eventually affects people in every other area.

Tolerance is essential! Tolerance means we must "live and let live." But it means more than that. It means we must "live and help live!" Jesus inhabited a prejudiced world of racial, cultural, national, and religious factions. The Pharisees and the Sadducees hated each other, and both of them hated the Gentiles, the Romans, and especially the

Samaritans. Yet Jesus made one of these despised heretical individuals the hero of his narrative.

Jesus was looking toward a world of increasing cultural and religious diversity when he told the wonderful story of the good Samaritan. The robbers in the story are obviously villains. Everyone knows what they did was wrong. Few cultures condone violence and theft. But there's more to the story: "Now by chance a priest was going down that road; and when he saw him, he passed by on the other side. So likewise a Levite, when he came to the place and saw him, passed by on the other side" (Luke 10:31–32).

Now, these men were not villains; they were upright citizens and religious leaders. But Jesus indicated that it isn't only thieves who hurt others; it's also people who are unconcerned and refuse to help others. The theme of the story is in the conclusion, which presents an unlikely and unexpected hero: "But a Samaritan while traveling came near him; and when he saw him, he was moved with pity. He went to him and bandaged his wounds, having poured oil and wine on them. Then he put him on his own animal, brought him to an inn, and took care of him. The next day he took out two denarii, gave them to the innkeeper, and said, 'Take care of him; and when I come back, I will repay you whatever more you spend'" (Luke 10:33–35).

This shocking twist probably caused a lot of anger. Jesus made respected men like priests and Levites look bad, and he made a disreputable man like the low-class Samaritan look good. The Samaritan was hated simply because of his unorthodox beliefs and worship practices. The Jews at that time believed the commandment "Love thy neighbor" meant only fellow Jews. They felt no obligation to love Gentiles or Samaritans.

Such bigotry is common even today. Some Christians read the Bible this way: "God so loves churchgoing, conservative, moral people like me." But it really says, "God so loved the world." That means the whole world—not just America, not just one race, not just Christians, but the whole world!

Why do you suppose Jesus told this story? What lessons can we learn from this parable? What point is he making about tolerance? First, Jesus is saying, "Don't hurt other people." The robbers were obviously evil and violent. They not only took what the man had; they beat him and left him to die. Their motto was, "What's yours is mine. I'll take it!" We don't know the race or religion of the robbers, but their actions are obviously wrong, both morally and legally. Even so, Jesus emphasizes that they aren't the only villains.

If Jesus were here today, he would not hurt people. "To do no harm" is the basis of the Hippocratic Oath taken by every medical doctor. It's obvious we must not be involved in murder or theft or violence. We may not be able to fix every problem in the world, but we can certainly avoid creating new ones or making the old ones worse. Almost every person, religious or not, would agree we should not hurt other people. Jesus would certainly not inflict harm.

Next, Jesus was saying, "Don't neglect other people." In a busy, crowded world, it's easy to shut our eyes and hearts to the problems around us. The priest and the Levite didn't actually steal or attack or inflict damage, but they did something just as bad. They overlooked another's pain and avoided the inconvenience of involvement. Their motto was, "What's mine is mine. I'll keep it!"

Now, these men were both religious leaders and temple employees, but they felt no empathy or sense of responsibility for a dying man. This shows the low level of spirituality in Jesus's day. They probably didn't even realize they had sinned, but James said, "Anyone, then, who knows the right thing to do and fails to do it, commits sin" (Jas 4:17). We will be judged not only on the bad we do, but also on the good we should have done and could have done but didn't do.

If Jesus were here today, he would not ignore other people's needs. Jesus would not be apathetic about social problems. He would be an active citizen, working for good legislation about issues such as poverty, child abuse, help for the elderly, the handicapped, and the victims of crime. He would be sensitive to others, and he would extend appropriate aid to the needy. The opposite of love isn't hatred;

it's apathy and indifference! Jesus would certainly not neglect the needy.

Finally, Jesus was saying, "Don't enable other people's indolence." This lesson teaches us how to be charitable and benevolent yet realistic. The Samaritan did something! He actually went the second mile. Helping others is helping Christ. Jesus said, "Just as you did it to one of the least of these who are members of my family, you did it to me" (Matt 25:40).

Nevertheless, we must set limits on our generosity. If Jesus were here today, he would not enable other people's indolence. Notice that the Samaritan delayed his journey and exerted physical effort and made a financial sacrifice, but it's important to note he didn't take on permanent responsibility for the injured man. He lent a hand in his misfortune, but he didn't promise to support him for the rest of his life. His motto was, "What's mine is ours. We'll share it!"

As Christians we must be kind, but we must also be realistic. We can't live other people's lives. We can't be overly indulgent to those who are irresponsible. Enabling people to continue in helplessness is wrong. Doing for others what they should be doing for themselves actually makes things worse. Jesus didn't go around handing out money to everyone he met then, and he wouldn't do that now if he were here.

If this were today, would Jesus advise us to pick up every hitchhiker and stop to change every stranded motorist's tire? Would he want us to take in every homeless person and give sandwiches to every hungry beggar? He would probably want us to support agencies that provide rehabilitation and training so these needy men and woman can become independent! He would emphasize the social principles of equality and compassion. In fact, he was far ahead of his time when it came to acceptance and tolerance. He even helped people who were different as to culture and belief. If Jesus lived today, he would be an unprejudiced, caring, and active citizen.

In the days following the Civil War, a Southern church was celebrating Communion. Surprisingly, an ex-slave went forward to receive the bread and wine. Many shocked and resentful white Christians remained in their pews. Then a well-known political leader went forward and knelt beside the black man. We are equal in the sight of God.

We're not sure how Jesus would react in every situation if he lived in America today, but we know empathy and concern would still be his main theme.

Chapter 12

Jesus Describes a Rebellious Son

A certain young man decided to live out the parable of the prodigal son. He squandered his money on alcohol, drugs, and prostitutes. When he was flat broke, he left his fair-weather friends and returned to his father. An acquaintance asked, "Well, when you came home, did your dad kill the fatted calf?"

"No!" the youth replied. "He didn't. But he almost killed the prodigal son."

That's not surprising. Most of us feel a need for retaliation and revenge. Jesus's story of the prodigal son is a classic analogy of the divine/human relationship. It overturns the traditional ideas about God. It tells us God is not a stern judge waiting to mete out punishment. God is not an authoritative dictator who forces people to obey. He loves us just as we are and encourages personal autonomy. He allows total freedom, and he forgives and accepts those who make mistakes. Above all, he offers second chances!

The prodigal son's problems were the inevitable result of his own poor choices and immature behavior. He hit bottom. Then he was finally ready to be realistic. At last he saw life as it really was! He made a rational decision to return home. What a wonderful and unexpected reception! His father didn't scold him and punish him. He didn't require an abject apology. He didn't even say, "I told you so." Instead, he loved and accepted him, just as he was. Giving him the "best robe" meant he was being reinstated to his original position with all the rights of a son. The ring symbolized the union of the father and son relationship. Giving him shoes showed he was not considered a slave.

The father's response is a dramatic illustration of grace. The older son showed no grace; he was jealous and bitter. This son typifies those self-righteous ones who obey out of fear, not love; who work out of duty, not concern. They follow all the legal rules, yet they condemn and judge others.

Why do you suppose Jesus told this surprising story about family relationships? What lessons can we learn from this parable? What point is he making about personal autonomy? First, Jesus emphasizes the importance of personal liberty. This father allowed his son to make a foolish decision. He didn't argue with him or criticize him. He didn't threaten to disinherit him. He didn't use shame or guilt to persuade him to stay. He loved him enough to let him go. We must realize that Jesus lived in a day when family and tribal solidarity were much more important than individual independence. That makes the father's attitude even more surprising. God doesn't force us to do anything.

If Jesus were here today, he would still encourage individual autonomy. In fact, he had been quite "autonomous" as a young boy of twelve when he stayed in the temple for three days. He showed his personal independence again when his family came to get him. By words and example Jesus was against enmeshment. Of course he loved his family and would want us to love our families, but not at the expense of our own independence and freedom of choice. Jesus would advocate personal liberty.

Next, Jesus emphasizes the importance of tough love. It's significant to note that when his son got into trouble, the father did not intervene or meddle. He didn't go into the far country to rescue him.

Instead, he let the boy reap the consequences of his decisions. When he hit bottom and wallowed in a pigpen, no one bailed him out. His father was wise enough to know that he had to "come to himself" and take action before he could be helped. It's important to note that Jesus didn't heal every sick person in Palestine. He only healed those who requested help. He even questioned one invalid's desire for health.

If Jesus were here today, he would still avoid controlling others. He never coerced or pressured anyone. This is demonstrated when he let the rich young ruler walk away. He didn't force change even when he knew people were making deadly decisions. Jesus never pressured or controlled others. He respected their autonomy, but he would advocate "tough love."

Finally, Jesus emphasized the importance of mercy. The father didn't condemn or punish the son when he returned. He welcomed him and even interrupted his apology. He was generous and joyous. He gave him all the symbols of sonship. Jesus wanted us to know that, as Christians, we are not slaves; we are sons and daughters of God.

If Jesus were here today, he would still be offering mercy. He never scolded or punished people who made mistakes. He even refused to condemn the woman caught in the act of adultery. On a more personal level, after Peter deserted him and lied and cursed, Jesus didn't shame or berate him. If this were today, we know Jesus would still encourage autonomy, practice tough love when necessary, and emphasize mercy.

Once, a man sat on a bus next to a miserable-looking youth who revealed he had just been released from prison. He had shamed his family, and they hadn't kept in touch. Now, however, he hoped they would forgive him. Afraid of rejection, he had written, suggesting that if his family wanted him back in their lives, they should tie a white ribbon in the big tree near the highway as a signal. If they didn't want him back, they were to do nothing; he would understand and stay on the bus and head west. As the bus neared his hometown, the suspense became so great that he couldn't bear to look out the window. The older man changed places with him and promised to watch for the tree. In a few minutes he touched the young convict's arm. "There it is," he whispered, "and it's all right. That whole tree is white with ribbons."

If Jesus were telling a modern story, would he use the plight of a rebellious teenager who became addicted to drugs and ended up homeless and destitute? Would he describe a young man who wasted his inheritance? Would he relate how an impulsive gambler lost the family fortune in Las Vegas? In a democracy we know citizens expect more individual freedom. Young people have many more options with college and travel, but some basic urges remain the same.

Even though the places and types of entertainment would be different if Jesus lived in America today, he would still emphasize individual freedom, tough love, and reconciliation.

Chapter 13

Jesus Rebukes a Selfish Miser

A shopper in a Christian bookstore saw a cap with the letters WWJD on it. The price tag read, "$16.99." When he asked what the letters stood for, the clerk responded, "It's a motto that asks, 'What would Jesus do?'"

The man looked at the cap again and replied, "Well, I don't know what he would do, but I know for sure one thing he wouldn't do. He wouldn't pay $16.99 for this cap!"

He's probably right. Jesus wasn't a spendthrift. He lived simply and had few possessions. He avoided waste. He used money; he didn't let money use him. Jesus told a dramatic, frightening story about a successful businessman:

> The land of a rich man produced abundantly. And he thought to himself, "What should I do, for I have no place to store my crops?" Then he said, "I will do this: I will pull down my barns and build larger ones, and there I will store all my grain and my goods. And I will say to my soul, Soul, you have ample goods laid up for many years; relax, eat, drink, be merry." But God said to him, "You fool! This very night your life

is being demanded of you. And the things you have prepared, whose will they be?" (Luke 12:16–20)

As far as we know, this man was not a criminal. There's no indication that he stole his wealth or even that he deprived or cheated others to obtain it. In fact, he seemed to be a hard worker and a good planner. He was ambitious and conservative, yet God called him a fool. He was self-centered. He claimed everything for himself alone. He forgot that he didn't have absolute control of his life. This miser had no gratitude. He was totally materialistic. His thoughts were about gratification of physical lusts. He didn't use any of his resources for others. He neglected spirituality. He wasn't "rich toward God."

Why do you suppose Jesus told such a negative and frightening illustration? What lessons can we learn from this parable? What point is he making about priorities? First, we must overcome selfishness. Personal survival and looking out for number one are universal human traits. Some self-interest is essential, but this man's only thought was about himself. Surprisingly, his belief or disbelief in God is not mentioned. Jesus would most likely agree with the writer who said, "Selfishness is the only real atheism!"

If Jesus lived today, he would still advocate moderation. He was not a fanatic. There's no indication that he was a beggar. He worked, and he would encourage us to work and earn a living. It's not money itself that's evil; it's the obsession to hoard money. Jesus wouldn't be selfish and greedy.

Next, we must overcome immediacy. Being impulsive and impatient are also universal human traits. People are prone to put *now* over *later* when it comes to getting what they want. "Deferred gratification" is not a natural characteristic; it must be developed. Jesus advised, "Do not store up for yourselves treasures on earth… but store up for yourselves treasures in heaven…. For where your treasure is, there your heart will be also" (Matt 6:19–21).

Unfortunately, this rich man's treasures were here on earth. He was more interested in possessions and pleasure than eternity. Recently, several elderly people were asked, "If you could live your life over, what would you do differently?" One answer dominated the results: "I'd do more things that would live on after my death." Most things that are really worthwhile take time. Paul said, "If we hope for what we do not see, we wait for it with patience" (Rom 8:25).

If Jesus lived today, he would still advocate deferred gratification. He would put first things first. Making more or having more should not be our main purpose in life. Being more, doing more, and giving more have much greater value. Good management is a Christian discipline. It's always wise to wait a few days before buying that "impulse item." Our financial statement is not the bottom line of our lives. Instead, what we would be worth if all our possessions and wealth were taken away is what really matters. Jesus wouldn't be impulsive and impatient.

Finally, we must overcome superficiality. Too often, we value the wrong things. Concrete items are more important to most of us than spiritual precepts. An interesting bit of gossip takes precedence over the consideration of a deeper concept. New gadgets get more of our attention than moral principles. These common tendencies are destructive, not because small talk and gadgets are evil, but because our time and resources are limited. Life is made up of choices. A yacht can cost more than four years in college. So before you buy one, be sure you can finance your children's education. A famous actor gave his wife a million-dollar diamond ring but didn't invest enough time or effort in strengthening their marriage to avoid divorce. We must decide what's really important.

Now, Jesus didn't say that eating and drinking and having fun were sins. In fact, the prodigal son's father did all three of these things when he welcomed his son home. Such things were a problem in the parable of the miser because they had become more important to him than wisdom, compassion, and spirituality. Paul said, "Set your minds on things that are above, not on things that are on earth" (Col 3:2). Jesus wouldn't be obsessed with superficial and trivial things.

If Jesus were here today, he would still advocate establishing important priorities. He would still be careful with his time and possessions and money. He would not waste his resources on a lavish lifestyle. Instead, he would use them to help people. Even so, he wouldn't give financial assistance in ways that destroy personal initiative. He would be a good steward of his resources. He wouldn't constantly think and dream and plan about how to make more money.

Once, a man suddenly received a large inheritance. He bought a beautiful home in the country, furnished it magnificently, hired a tutor for his children, and invited many friends to a sumptuous housewarming. During the housewarming the rich man observed that the tutor was drinking too much and singing bawdy songs. The master of the house was angry to see this kind of behavior from one of his employees. He called the tutor aside and said, "Cool it, man, and don't forget that your time in this house is limited."

The tutor, slightly inebriated, replied, "What about you, sir? Don't forget that your time in this house is also limited." That's what Jesus was saying. Since our time on this earth is limited, we must use our resources in a productive way.

Now, if this were today, would Jesus tell a modern story about a man who is a day trader in the stock market? Would he relate the details of a lucrative business deal? Would he describe a woman whose music video made her a wealthy star overnight? Would he remind people of tragic movie stars and powerful executives? We can't know exactly which rich and famous person Jesus would use as an illustration, but we do know there are many "rich fools" in our world. Even though Jesus would describe a different individual if he lived in America today, his general principles about materialism would still be the same.

Chapter 14

Jesus Warns about Self-Righteousness

An interesting cartoon shows a princess in her crown and beautiful robe talking to a prince decked out in a uniform. She looks disgusted and, with her hands on her hips, says, "I think I liked you better as a frog!" There's a lot of truth in that statement. People with their humanity showing usually have more friends than those who appear to be perfect. Self-righteous behavior and "holier than thou" attitudes turn us off.

Jesus encouraged us to be realistic and nonjudgmental. Self-righteousness is deadly. It never helps us, and it always hurts others. Jesus told a story about two people who exemplify arrogance and humility (see Luke 18:10–11). These individuals represent the best and the worst in that society. Pharisees were extremely religious and extremely moral. They were upright citizens and loyal worshipers. The tax collectors or publicans, on the other hand, were despised as henchmen of the hated Romans. They were seen as traitors and lawbreakers. But Jesus gave a strange twist to his description: "The Pharisee, standing by himself, was praying thus, 'God, I thank you that I am not like other people: thieves, rogues, adulterers, or even like this tax collector. I fast twice a week; I give a tenth of all my income" (Luke 18:11–12).

Now, this man was not lying. He was probably describing his behavior and lifestyle truthfully. He did obey all these commandments, but he was also proud and conceited. He didn't mingle with "sinners." His prayer included no expressions of intercession or gratitude or confession. Jesus despised such self-righteousness and arrogance. These people would stand out on the street corner broadcasting the amount of their offering. Imagine someone jumping up in church and saying, "Hey, everybody! Look how much I'm putting in the plate today."

They would gather crowds to hear their unending, holier-than-thou prayers. They fasted publicly. Can't you just hear them saying, "I haven't had anything to eat all day" or "Thank you for inviting me to lunch, but I'm fasting"?

Also, they were pious talkers and cliché users. Jesus called it "vain repetition." We still have a lot of such religious jargon. People say, "Praise the Lord," "Amen and amen," and "Blessed Jesus" whether these statements make any sense or not. These may sound like "spiritual" phrases, but years of overuse have made them meaningless.

The publican was different. The scripture says, "The tax collector, standing far off, would not even look up to heaven, but was beating his breast and saying, 'God, be merciful to me, a sinner!'" (Luke 18:13). The publican's prayer was much shorter and much simpler; it contains only seven words. But Jesus said, "I tell you, this man went down to his home justified rather than the other" (Luke 18:14).

Why do you suppose Jesus contrasted the publican and the Pharisee so dramatically? What lessons can we learn from this parable? What point is he making about self-righteousness? First, Jesus advocates emotional honesty. The publican was aware of his own sins and sincere in admitting his flaws, but the Pharisee was in denial. He only mentioned his strengths, not his weaknesses. However, no one is perfect. John said, "If we say that we have no sin, we deceive ourselves, and the truth is not in us" (1 John 1:8).

If Jesus were here today, he would still require emotional honesty. He said God doesn't look at the outside. He looks inwardly, and so must we. We have a tendency to fool ourselves by thinking we act from one motive when we're really acting from a different one. This is called rationalization. But it's not simply our pious words or our charitable deeds that count. It's our attitudes and our motives. Jesus would stress authenticity and sincerity.

Next, Jesus denounced negative comparisons. The publican wasn't critical of fellow worshipers. He gave no excuses, and he assigned no blame. He was praying to God. The Pharisee was too busy justifying himself and judging others to worship God. Such pride is a sin. It consists of comparing our strengths to other people's weaknesses. Isn't it interesting that the Pharisee compared himself to a lowly publican instead of to Abraham or Moses? We seem to always notice those who are "worse" than we are. Paul warns us, however, "You have no excuse, whoever you are, when you judge others; for in passing judgment on another you condemn yourself, because you, the judge, are doing the very same things" (Rom 2:1). If Jesus were here today, he would still forbid negative comparisons. We are all brothers in the flesh, so it's not profitable or appropriate to boast and brag. Jesus would stress humility and tolerance.

Finally, Jesus insisted on personal accountability. We can't change other people. Furthermore, we're not responsible for solving their problems. Nowhere does the Bible tell us we must fix others or that we will be held responsible for their sins. Instead, it reads, "The parents shall not be put to death for the children, or the children be put to death for the parents; but all shall be put to death for their own sins" (2 Kgs 14:6).

The publican was concerned about his own spiritual condition and his own self-improvement. The Pharisee was interested only in pointing fingers. If Jesus were here today, he would still insist on self-examination. He spoke to this issue in blunt language, saying, "For with the judgment you make you will be judged, and the measure you give will be the measure you get. Why do you see the speck in your neighbor's eye, but do not notice the log in your own eye? Or how can you say to your neighbor, 'Let me take the speck out of your eye,' while the log is in your own eye? You hypocrite, first take the log out of your own eye, and then you will see clearly to take the speck out of your neighbor's eye" (see Matt 7:2–5).

We really begin to grow as Christians when we realize the roots of most of our problems are not in our families, our friends, or our business associates. Most of the roots of our problems are within us. Jesus would stress personal accountability and diligence. We know Jesus would not be a pious, self-righteous snob. He was never known for his sanctimonious speech. He was never known for his moralistic behavior. Instead, he was known for his compassion and tolerance. He even broke religious laws to help hurting people.

According to legend, a famous biblical scholar appeared at the pearly gates seeking admission. St. Peter said, "I don't see your name on my list."

"Oh, it must be there," the man replied. "I'm the one who wrote all those religious books."

"Sorry, but I'm afraid they're not recorded."

"But I'm the one who delivered those popular lectures on spirituality," the man continued.

St. Peter just shook his head. Shoulders drooping, the scholar turned and began to walk away. Suddenly, St. Peter's face brightened. "Wait a minute," he called after him. "Are you that fellow who built those little birdhouses and put out seed for the birds every winter?"

"Why, yes, that's me," the man answered.

"Oh, then forgive me," said St. Peter. "Of course we have a place for you."

The point of this little myth about rewards is that great deeds done for show are worthless; small acts of kindness done for love are rewarded.

If Jesus told a modern story, would he compare the worship practices of a prostitute and a missionary? Would he contrast the attitudes of a bartender with an evangelist? Would he reveal the inner motives of an alcoholic and a church leader? We don't know for sure who he would use in his illustrations. But we do know he would look beneath the surface. He wouldn't evaluate by superficial words and actions.

Even though Jesus would be dealing with different races and occupations if he lived in America today, his attitude about hypocrisy and self-righteousness would still be the same.

Chapter 15

Jesus Gives Advice about Productivity

Three hikers came upon a raging river. The first guy prayed, "Please, God, give me the strength to cross this river." Poof! God gave him strong arms and legs, and he swam across.

The second guy prayed, "Please, God, give me the ability to cross this river." Poof! God gave him a boat, and he rowed across.

The third guy saw how it worked and prayed, "God, give me the knowledge to cross this river." Poof! God gave him a map that showed a nearby bridge, and he walked across the river.

We all have different gifts. Jesus told a wonderful story about various levels of talents and resources. He said, "It is as if a man, going on a journey, summoned his slaves and entrusted his property to them; to one he gave five talents, to another two, to another one, to each according to his ability. Then he went away" (Matt 25:14–15).

It is important for people to achieve all they can with what they do have. Jesus was clear about that in the parable of the talents. He described how the man who had been given five talents and the man who had been given two talents both immediately began productive plans of action. Unfortunately, the man who had been given one talent refused to use it. He chose a totally unproductive course (see

Matt 25:16–18). For a while, all three seemed to go on as before. Nevertheless, there would be consequences of these choices. We may not reap what we sow immediately, but we will reap what we sow eventually.

Jesus complimented both of the productive servants, but the response to the unproductive servant was unexpectedly harsh and final (see Matt 25:20–25). This servant made several mistakes: He had a negative evaluation of his master; he made excuses and projected blame; above all, he was negligent and unproductive. In turn, his master's reply was critical (see Matt 25:26–30).

Why do you suppose Jesus told this story? What lessons can we learn from this parable? What point was he making about productivity? First, Jesus emphasized that everyone has a gift. Every human being has some ability or some strength or some resource. There are no totally useless people. In this parable Jesus didn't even mention a no-talent person because they don't exist. Many people feel they are being humble and modest when they claim, "I have no special talents; I can't do anything well." But that's simply an excuse to avoid responsibility. God doesn't create worthless things. Peter says, "Serve one another with whatever gift each of you has received" (1 Pet 4:10).

If Jesus were here today, he would still hold every person responsible for some contribution. Jesus knew that human beings' lives are destroyed when they are allowed to sit idly by and do nothing. He would be pleased with dedicated teachers, doctors, and ministers. But he would be equally pleased with hard-working dishwashers and gardeners and childcare workers. Everyone can do something productive. Jesus had enormous respect for those who do small things: "Whoever gives even a cup of cold water to one of these little ones…. None of these will lose their reward" (Matt 10:42). Jesus would expect everyone to use the abilities and resources they have.

Next, Jesus showed that productivity will be rewarded. He wanted to assure us that there is no difference in the rewards of those who have a lot and use it well and those who have much less but use it well. Ordinary men and women shouldn't be jealous or envious of superstars or multitalented individuals. There are no inferior human beings. Little kindnesses are important. Jesus praised the woman who washed his feet and promised rewards to those who gave away cups of water. He said those who fed the hungry and housed the stranger and made clothes for the poor and visited the sick were blessed and welcomed into heaven (see Matt 25:34–36).

If Jesus were here today, he would still value productivity. We will be judged by what we do with what we have! The small contributions of those who only have a few talents but use them well will be honored just as much as the great contributions of the rich and famous. Remember his remarks about the widow:

> [Jesus] sat down opposite the treasury, and watched the crowd putting money into the treasury. Many rich people put in large sums. A poor widow came and put in two small copper coins, which are worth a penny. Then he called his disciples and said to them, "Truly I tell you, this poor widow has put in more than all those who are contributing to the treasury. For all of them have contributed out of their abundance; but she out of her poverty has put in everything she had, all she had to live on." (Mark 12:41–44)

Jesus would assure us that God blesses those who share their money, talent, and time with others.

Finally, Jesus indicated that indolence will be punished. If we're apathetic and idle, not only will we lose our reward, but we will even lose the ability or the resource itself. It's a true demonstration of the "use it or lose it" principle. It seemed almost unfair to take the little bit the third man had away from him, but that's how life works. Jesus did not mince words about indolence and idleness: "Every tree that does not bear good fruit is cut down and thrown into the fire" (Matt 7:19).

If Jesus were here today, he would still condemn apathy and laziness. He wouldn't accept excuses from those who do nothing. Our lack of ability or our tough breaks in the past do not exempt us from making our contribution now. Productivity requires action. A recipe book doesn't feed anyone. A blueprint doesn't build anything. A road map doesn't go anywhere. We must act! Jesus worked with his hands and his head and his heart. He was constantly teaching, healing, and counseling. If he lived today, he would still use his abilities in productive ways.

A minister told of a woman who had polio. He said, "She's in a wheelchair. She can't even feed herself. But she's an exciting, enthusiastic person who thinks about others. For instance, right now, she is busy reading law books to a blind student. That's her current project. She can't even use her hands. Instead, she has this long object that she holds in her mouth to flip the pages. The student she is helping will soon graduate as a lawyer, and he'll go out and help people solve their problems. He is able to get his education, even though he is totally blind, because one woman reads all his books to him. This proves that no matter how 'handicapped' you are, you can do something."

Now, if this were today, would Jesus use billionaires and middle-class professionals and day laborers as examples? Would he talk about a person with a genius-level IQ and an average man or woman and a mentally challenged individual? Would he hold the ordinary citizen who can only do a few simple tasks accountable for using those few abilities? Would he hold the multitalented performer who can sing and entertain and do many things accountable for using his many abilities?

Yes, that's the point of this story. He didn't expect the man with one talent to gain as much as the man with two talents or the man with five talents. But he did expect him to do something! Jesus wouldn't scorn a street cleaner and honor a world leader. We know Jesus would use modern language and current situations to illustrate this lesson if he lived in America today, but his principles concerning productivity would still be the same.

Chapter 16

Jesus Encourages the Use of Opportunities

Once, a family visited the ocean. Everyone enjoyed swimming and playing in the waves except one little boy. Nobody could persuade him to touch the water. Finally, on the last day, just before they left, he ventured in. It was wonderful! He loved it. Unfortunately, it was time to leave. "Oh, Mom!" he wailed. "Why didn't you make me go in before?"

Sometimes we refuse to take advantage of opportunities until it's too late. That's partly because "opportunities" aren't always labeled as such. Sometimes they come in the form of obstacles, challenges, or even aggravations. It's important to recognize and take advantage of our opportunities.

Jesus used a common social occasion to teach a life lesson. In those days, rich people and rulers often had banquets. They were planned to celebrate births or weddings or military victories. It was a great honor to receive an invitation to such an event. But, as usual, Jesus gave this story a strange twist: "The kingdom of heaven may be compared to a king who gave a wedding banquet for his son. He sent his slaves to call those who had been invited to the wedding banquet, but they would not come" (Matt 22:2–3).

The host couldn't believe this unreasonable response, so he tried again, adding details about the lavish meal and preparations. Again, his gracious invitation was ignored. In fact, some became downright rude and even violent. In turn, the king responded aggressively (see Matt 22:4–8). We can't really blame the king for his reaction. Those who neglected this once-in-a-lifetime opportunity didn't deserve to be entertained. However, his next act is surprising: "'Go therefore into the main streets, and invite everyone you find to the wedding banquet.' Those slaves went out into the streets and gathered all whom they found, both good and bad; so the wedding hall was filled with guests" (Matt 22:9–10).

Why do you suppose Jesus chose this subject for discussion? What lessons can we learn from this parable? What point was he making about opportunity? First, we must recognize our opportunities. Jesus began his ministry by offering a generous message of hope and grace to the religious Pharisees, but they did not recognize its importance and refused to listen. When we refuse to listen, we may be missing out on a great experience. We may be rejecting a wonderful gift. We may regret our decision for the rest of our lives. Felix had a wonderful opportunity when Paul witnessed to him, but he didn't respond (see Acts 24:25). As far as we know, Felix never had another chance. Sometimes opportunity only knocks once. Since we may not get a second chance, we need to rearrange our priorities and do the most important things first.

If Jesus were here today, he would advise us to recognize our opportunities. That might be difficult since opportunities often look like extra work or frustrating problems. Of course, since we can't do everything, responding to an opportunity may cost us something. Since our time and energy and resources are limited, we'll probably have to give up other interests and pleasures in order to respond. That's why making decisions is so hard. That's why many people make the wrong choices, but Jesus said when we see something of value, we may have to sacrifice in order to obtain it (see Matt 13:45–46).

Next, we must appreciate our opportunities. To do this, we must get our priorities straight. We must make wise decisions. We must choose between good or better and between better or best. We must avoid excuses. One wise man said, "An excuse is a lie in disguise." If Jesus were here today, he would still advise us to appreciate our opportunities. We're fortunate to have so many choices as to occupations, leisure activities, and worship. We take too many things for granted. We expect to always have numerous options and possibilities. We think we'll always be able to earn a living. We think we'll always be able to buy what we please. We think we'll always be able to enjoy recreation. We think we'll always be able to worship as we choose. We think we'll always be able to follow Jesus. But these circumstances could change overnight.

Finally, we must take advantage of our opportunities. It's important to recognize and appreciate our opportunities, but we must also act. We must not delay, because some opportunities have time limits. The door may close. The offer may be withdrawn. The possibility will not be available forever. In the story of the five foolish virgins, Jesus showed the danger of delaying preparation. The foolish ones did not take any oil with them, and when the bridegroom came, those unprepared girls were left behind. These girls missed their opportunity. When they did get ready, it was too late. Likewise, we're not indispensable. Others can take our place!

If Jesus were here today, he would still advise us to take advantage of our opportunities. The poet J. T. Bolding wrote,

> Waste not the opportunities
> That come from day to day.
> Just make the most of everyone,
> You'll not pass again this way.

If this were today, Jesus would still use every opportunity for service. Too many of us miss or ignore our opportunities. According to legend, a very old man was sitting in his hut outside the city of Bethlehem. A boy came running up and said, "Ishmael, I just heard that you were one of the shepherds on the hill many years ago when

Jesus was born. Tell me, what did the baby look like?" The old man's eyes misted. His lips trembled as he answered, "Yes, I was with those shepherds. I did hear about a baby, but I was tired that night, and I didn't bother to go. I never had another chance to see him." This man missed his only opportunity!

If Jesus told a modern story, would he use the example of a person declining a once-in-a-lifetime invitation to a dinner at the White House? Would he tell of a man who rejected a fabulous job offer from a great organization? Would he tell of a young student refusing a scholarship to a famous university? What kind of excuses would modern men and women give? Benjamin Franklin said, "He that's good at making excuses is seldom good for anything else."

Of course we don't know the specific details Jesus would describe. Even though he would use different examples if he lived in America today, his general attitude regarding opportunities would still be the same.

Chapter 17

Jesus Finally Loses His Temper

A university coach once sent his assistant to do some recruiting. The assistant asked, "What kind of player are we looking for?"

The coach replied, "Well, there's the fellow that you knock down and he stays down."

The assistant said, "We don't want him, do we?"

"That's right," the coach said.

"Then there's the fella that you knock him down and he gets up, you knock him down and he gets up, you knock him down and he gets up."

"Oh!" the assistant said. "Now, that's the guy we want, isn't it, Coach?"

"No," said the coach. "We want that guy who keeps knocking everybody down."

Well, some violence might be acceptable in football, but in real life it can be destructive. Of course, there is such a thing as righteous indignation, but ninety-nine percent of the time our rage is not righteous. Instead, it's the result of personal pride and selfishness.

Jesus didn't show anger often, but when he did, it was usually directed at judgmental religious leaders who hurt people. Once, when he was healing a cripple on the sabbath, the Pharisees were critical. Jesus asked them, "'Is it lawful to do good or to do harm on the sabbath, to save life or to kill?' But they were silent. He looked around at them with anger; he was grieved at their hardness of heart" (Mark 3:45).

He also became angry one day in Jerusalem. In fact, his anger had been smoldering for a long time. The greed and hypocrisy of the entire religious establishment became symbolized in this temple confrontation. Every Gospel relates this incident. Matthew and Luke give brief accounts: "[Jesus] entered the temple and began to drive out those who were selling things there; and he said, 'It is written, "My house shall be a house of prayer"; but you have made it a den of robbers'" (Luke 19:45–46).

Mark adds a few details: "And he entered the temple and began to drive out those who were selling and those who were buying in the temple, and he overturned the tables of the money changers and the seats of those who sold doves; and he would not allow anyone to carry anything through the temple. He was teaching and saying, 'Is it not written, "My house shall be called a house of prayer for all the nations"? But you have made it a den of robbers'" (Mark 11:15–17).

John's narrative gives the most information: "The Passover of the Jews was near, and Jesus went up to Jerusalem. In the temple he found people selling cattle, sheep, and doves, and the money changers seated at their tables. Making a whip of cords, he drove all of them out of the temple, both the sheep and the cattle. He also poured out the coins of the money changers and overturned their tables. He told those who were selling the doves, 'Take these things out of here! Stop making my Father's house a marketplace!'" (John 2:13–16).

Jesus always despised greed and deceit, but he especially despised the misuse of the people's place of worship. For the merchants in the temple, Passover offered financial opportunities for those who bought and sold. The peasants' money was different from the temple money and necessitated a change, giving rise to a tremendous black market. Because they offered sacrifices, these merchants would stock every available cage and pen with pigeons, cattle, and sheep to be sold at inflated prices.

Jesus's visit to the temple and his response to this age-old custom must have taken everyone by surprise. Not only was it the act of a man who had been confronting hypocrisy for years; it was also the act of a courageous man who knew only too well the consequences of such actions.

Why do you suppose Jesus reacted in this very uncharacteristic way in the temple? What lesson can we learn from this incident? What point does it make about confrontation? First, Jesus's anger had a just cause. Jesus wasn't resorting to violence over a trivial aggravation or a personal confrontation. He wasn't trying to protect his own ego or even his life. Instead, reverence for God's house and concern over the oppression of the poor and the alienated led to his attack. He had nothing to gain personally. Instead, he had much to lose. The religious leaders immediately began making plans to kill him.

His actions were for others, especially for "the least of these." He was acting for the helpless and disenfranchised. Jesus was angered by the exorbitant prices forced upon the hapless worshipers. His own parents had been in that position when they presented him as an infant in the temple. He was also angered by the use of the temple as a marketplace—sheep bleating, vendors hawking their wares, the noise and smell everywhere—in a place intended for meditation and prayers. Even more, he was angered by what these men were teaching. They were insinuating that the bribery of perfect sacrifices was the right way to God.

If Jesus were here today, he would still try to protect the victims of society. The children, the poor, the elderly, and the minorities would be his special concern. He was passionate about the helpless ones who had no political voice and little financial power. He said, "If any of you put a stumbling block before one of these little ones who believe in me, it would be better for you if a great millstone were fastened around your neck and you were drowned in the depths of the sea" (Matt 18:6). A nation is evaluated by how it treats the very old, the very young, and the least of these. Jesus's anger was justified because he saw helpless people being abused.

Next, Jesus used violence as a last resort. In the temple that day, nothing else would have gained attention and effected change. Jesus had taught and served and ministered to these people for three years with little success. Words wouldn't do. From his first visit to Jerusalem at the age of twelve to the end of his earthly life, Jesus was upset by what he saw and heard there. Several times he had expressed his frustration at people's obstinance, saying, "You faithless and perverse generation, how much longer must I be with you? How much longer must I put up with you?" (Matt 17:17). Later he said, "Jerusalem, Jerusalem…how often have I desired to gather your children together as a hen gathers her brood under her wings, and you were not willing!" (Matt 23:37). None of the religious leaders had changed their attitudes or actions.

If Jesus were here today, he would still try everything else first. He would teach, advise, and warn, but if words didn't work, he would take some kind of action. He would agree with Paul, who said, "If it is possible, so far as it depends on you, live peaceably with all" (Rom 12:18).

Unfortunately, reality tells us that sometimes peace is not possible. It took a revolution to free America. It took a civil war to end slavery. It took military action to eradicate Hitler's holocaust. Sometimes such methods are necessary, but they should be last resorts, because they always hurt innocent people and cause needless destruction. Jesus had taught for three years without results, so his angry actions in the temple were a last resort.

Finally, Jesus didn't abuse individuals. In this case, he was overthrowing a system. The money and the materialistic paraphernalia were the targets of his anger. It was a case of hating the sin but still loving the sinner. Even when a disciple cut off the ear of a guard who had come to arrest him, Jesus said, "'No more of this.' And he touched his ear and healed him" (Luke 22:51). Jesus always practiced what he preached. He said, "Love your enemies and pray for those who persecute you, so that you may be children of your Father in heaven" (Matt 5:44–45). He even prayed for those who crucified him (see Luke 23:34).

If Jesus were here today, he would still be angry at injustice. He would dismantle illegal and immoral institutions that promote schemes to defraud helpless men, women, and children. Unscrupulous televangelist appeals, dishonorable business practices, and unfair government programs would be targeted. Jesus especially warned against violence to individuals. He said, "Do not resist an evildoer. But if anyone strikes you on the right cheek, turn the other also.... Love your enemies and pray for those who persecute you" (Matt 5:39, 44). Jesus would never retaliate against individuals for personal reasons, but he would try to abolish corrupt systems.

If this were today, we know Jesus would still take action to ensure fairness for all. Over the centuries many people have come to watershed moments when confrontation with evil was absolutely essential. Martin Luther came to such a place. When he confronted a corrupt religious establishment, he said, "Here I stand. I can do no other!" There comes a time in each of our lives when we have to stand for something. There comes a time when inaction is a sin. James said, "Anyone, then, who knows the right thing to do and fails do it, commits sin" (Jas 4:17).

If Jesus were here now, would he destroy the lavish headquarters of some televangelist who had cheated the elderly? Would he attack extortion in high places? Would he expose deceitful business scams? We don't know where or how he would make a stand if he lived today in America, but he would still try to eliminate the same evils.

Chapter 18

Jesus Faces a Personal Crisis

One day, a farmer hired a man and asked him to paint the barn. He did it in one day. Next he asked him to cut up a pile of wood. Again, he did it in one day. Then he asked the man to sort a pile of potatoes into two groups: one box that was good enough to sell and one box to feed the hogs.

At the end of the day, he went to check on the man and found that he hadn't even started. He asked, "What on earth is the matter? You've always been such a fast worker!"

The man shook his head and replied, "Sure, Boss. Work I can do, but it's these decisions that are killing me!"

Decisions are hard, and sooner or later all of us have to face them. Jesus made a lot of choices during his life and ministry. He faced three crucial temptations immediately after his baptism. When he preached his first sermon in Nazareth, saying that God blessed foreigners rather than Israelites, his own neighbors were furious and tried to kill him. The scripture says, "When they heard this, all in the synagogue were filled with rage. They got up, drove him out of the town, and led him to the brow of the hill on which their town was built, so that they might hurl him off the cliff" (Luke 4:28–29).

Many times, he experienced hostility and threats. Once he faced his enemies, saying, "Why are you looking for an opportunity to kill me?" (John 7:19). When he compared himself to Abraham, his life was again threatened (see John 8:59). Jesus was well aware that his mission would eventually require a sacrifice (see, e.g., John 10:14–15).

Even his disciples knew there was danger. When he decided to go back to Judea after Lazarus's death, they cautioned against his decision (see John 11:8). When he attempted to prepare his followers for the coming tragedy, Peter especially protested (see Matt 16:21–22).

Now he had finally come to a crisis that demanded an immediate life-or-death decision. The scriptures say, "They went to a place called Gethsemane; and he said to his disciples, 'Sit here while I pray.' He took with him Peter and James and John, and began to be distressed and agitated. And he said to them, 'I am deeply grieved, even to death; remain here, and keep awake'" (Mark 14:32–34).

Notice that Jesus was open and honest and emotional. He admitted to his closest friends that he was depressed and miserable, saying, "Abba, Father, for you all things are possible; remove this cup from me; yet, not what I want, but what you want" (Mark 14:36). He prayed alone, and no one is sure how the Gospel writers knew what he said since the only witnesses were asleep. But Jesus prayed again and again, wrestling with a deeply momentous decision.

Why do you suppose Jesus showed such human emotions in the garden of Gethsemane? What lessons can we learn from this incident? What point does it make about facing a crisis? First, Jesus needed spiritual guidance. Most dedicated Christians really want to do God's will, but during those low moments when we need him most, it's hard to feel God's presence. Jesus had to pray three times before he could determine God's will (see Luke 22:41–42). Even though he had prayed this prayer of commitment, on the cross he felt totally abandoned and rejected. In despair he cried out, "My God, my God, why have you forsaken me?" (Matt 27:46).

If Jesus were here today, he would still need spiritual guidance. He expressed this often, saying, "I do nothing on my own, but I speak these things as the Father instructed me" (John 8:28). Life is complex. No one has perfect knowledge about the best responses. There are no divine messages written in the sky. There are no audible spiritual voices giving instruction. It's significant that at this moment of decision, Jesus used the same methods available to us to discern God's will. He used prayer!

Jesus also had an intellectual knowledge of the scriptures. He had an emotional connection with the Holy Spirit. He had a physical evaluation of circumstances. What we know, what we feel, and what we observe gives us a triple check when making decisions. At this crucial moment Jesus heeded spiritual guidance.

Next, Jesus needed people to support him. All of us need family and friends; unfortunately, even our best friends will often let us down. Many times, Jesus's followers left when he taught unpopular beliefs. In fact, they often left him in droves. At this crucial time in Jesus's life, even his intimate followers went to sleep. If Jesus were here today, he would still need a support group. People need people. All of us derive strength and comfort from those around us.

A man was visiting Sequoia National Park. The guide pointed out a tree that stands over two hundred feet high and has a circumference of seventy feet. It has stood in California for almost two thousand years. A tourist from West Texas—where the mesquite trees are like scrubby, overgrown bushes—was speechless as he stood there drinking in the sequoia's majesty. "I bet the roots on that tree are a hundred feet deep," he remarked to the guide.

"No, sir," the guide responded. "As a matter of fact, sequoia trees have roots just barely under the ground."

"That's impossible!" the man exclaimed. "I'm a country boy, and I know better than that. If the roots don't grow deep into the earth, strong winds will blow the trees over."

"Not sequoia trees. They only grow in clusters, and their roots intertwine with each other under the surface of the earth. So when the strong winds come, they hold each other up."

That's exactly what family and friends and church members do for each other. They provide a caring group to hold each other up. Jesus needed his friends. At this crucial moment Jesus needed human support.

Finally, Jesus needed personal courage. Finding God's will is important, but it's not the last word. Our support group helps a lot, but it can only go so far. The final moment of commitment is up to us. We often have to struggle with tough decisions and then stand absolutely alone in that decision. When Jesus stood before Pilate, not one follower was there to support him. Jesus knew a verbal defense was useless. If Jesus were here today, he would still need personal courage.

Sometimes, even when we know what to do, we don't want to do it. Winston Churchill, when facing Nazi Germany, said, "However tempting it might be when trouble lies ahead to step aside, but I do not intend to take that cowardly course. On the contrary, I intend to stand at my post and persevere with my duty as I see it." Shakespeare said, "Cowards die many times before their deaths. The valiant never taste of death but once."

Once, a little girl stood facing her older brother and his buddy. "Give me back my doll," she demanded. The boys had snatched it from her stroller and were holding it hostage behind their fort.

"Come get her," they teased. She waited with a tearful face, unable to muster the courage to retrieve her doll.

Just then, a car pulled into the driveway and a tall man got out. A minute later the frustrated child showed up at the fort with her daddy right behind her. This time she spoke with authority: "Now, give me my doll!"

It was instantly returned.

What a change in that little girl's confidence. Now, she was relying on the presence of her father. It's the same with us. When we face a crisis that requires more strength and courage and coping ability than we feel we have, we can have faith that our heavenly Father is with us.

If Jesus were here today, would he try to find a quiet place to pray? Would he take some friends with him? Would he agonize over hard choices? We can't know details, but if Jesus lived in America today, his response to a personal crisis would still be the same.

Chapter 19

Jesus Offers Reconciliation

Once, a very disobedient little boy said, "Please go away, Mom. I'm talking to God."

"But isn't there something you need to tell me?" his mother asked.

"No!" he quickly answered. "You'll just fuss and fuss, but God will forgive me and forget about it."

God does forgive and forget (see Jer 31:34; Ps 103:12; 1 John 1:9). Jesus did that with Peter. In fact, he did more than that. He reinstated him and entrusted him with a great responsibility. After Jesus was arrested, Peter lied and cursed and denied that he knew him. When Peter realized what he had done, he probably thought he could never be forgiven (see Matt 26:69–75).

In fact, the whole gospel movement seemed to be over. Peter gave up. He went back to his old way of life. Later, when Jesus appeared to the disciples, it's significant that Peter was the first to respond. Usually, when we're guilty and ashamed, we try to avoid the person we've hurt, but Peter wanted to see Jesus. Jesus fed the group because he knew they were feeling confused and uncertain, and eating together helped break the ice (see John 21:7–17). Peter had denied Jesus three times, so he was given an opportunity to declare his loyalty three times. After Peter's statements of commitment, Jesus said, "Follow me" (John 21:19).

Why do you suppose Jesus interacted with Peter as he did? What lessons can we learn from this incident? What point does it make about the hope for reconciliation? First, Jesus showed that reconciliation and restoration are possible. After lying and denying Jesus, Peter was still able to preach that historic sermon at Pentecost (see Acts 2:14). He began to preach, and afterward thousands were converted (see Acts 2:41). Peter went on to lead the church in the first century.

David believed in God's mercy to sinners. After his sin with Bathsheba, he said, "Restore to me the joy of your salvation, and sustain in me a willing spirit" (Ps 51:12). No matter how low we fall or how badly we fail, we can always come back.

If Jesus were here today, he would still restore fellowship. He never gives up on a person. He encourages us to never give up until every lost sheep is found (Luke 15:4). Peter actually referred to this parable, saying, "You were going astray like sheep, but now you have returned to the shepherd and guardian of your souls" (1 Pet 2:25).

Next, Jesus showed that reconciliation requires a recommitment. Jesus didn't criticize, condemn, shame, or punish Peter. As far as we know, the dreadful incident in Pilate's court was never mentioned again. But he did give Peter the opportunity to make a recommitment. Three times, Jesus asked, "Do you love me?" And three times Peter answered, "Yes!"

Later, Peter expressed it this way: "The God of all grace, who has called you to his eternal glory in Christ, will himself restore, support, strengthen, and establish you" (1 Pet 5:10). He knew this from personal experience.

If Jesus were here today, he would still accept a fallen person without condemnation. He wouldn't criticize and shame him. He wouldn't say, "I told you so." He wouldn't withhold affirmation and make him suffer. Such a negative response does no good. The sinner already knows he is weak. He is already aware of his failure. He already feels guilty. Instead, Jesus would accept and validate the fallen one. He would practice what he preached when he said, "Be merciful, just as your Father is merciful" (Luke 6:36). Jesus would show that reconciliation requires repentance and recommitment.

Finally, Jesus showed that reconciliation includes a mission. The best evidence of repentance is behavior. The best cure for backsliding is service. When Jesus gave Peter a mission to accomplish, he was showing that he still had faith in him and that he still valued his contributions. Three times, Peter was commanded to feed the sheep. This meant he was to work and minister to and teach the people.

Jeremiah also believed sinners could return to service. He said, "Therefore thus says the LORD: If you turn back, I will take you back" (Jer 15:19). We are not saved to sit; we are saved to serve! If Jesus were here today, he would still give those who had sinned and repented a new mission. This would show trust and give them a standard to live up to. That's the best way to rehabilitate anyone. If you treat a person as he has been, he'll remain that way. But if you treat a person as he can be, he'll become that. God gives people second chances.

Peter was given a second chance. Jesus would show that reconciliation includes a purpose and a mission.

Now, if this were today, we know that Jesus would still be a confirmed reconciler. He wouldn't hold us to our past. A wise man said, "The most meaningless statistic in a ballgame is the score at halftime."

Years ago, two university teams were playing in the Rose Bowl. During the second quarter, one player recovered a fumble for his team. But then he became confused and ran sixty-five yards in the wrong direction. A teammate had to tackle him to prevent him from scoring for the opposing team.

At halftime, the men filed into the dressing room, and all of them sat down on the benches, except the embarrassed young man who had goofed. He crouched in the corner. A coach usually has a lot to say during halftime, but that day the coach was silent. Finally, just before game time, the coach looked at the team and said, "Men, the same team that started the first half will start the second."

The youth didn't budge. Instead, he looked up and said, "Coach, I can't do it. I've ruined you. I've ruined the university. I've ruined myself. I can't face that crowd."

But the coach put his hand on the boy's shoulder and said, "Son, get up and go on back. The game is only half over."

He did go back, and spectators said they had never seen a man play football like he played that second half.

All of us have run in the wrong direction. All of us have fumbled and fallen. All of us have regrets and shame. But Jesus would say, "Get up and go on. The game is only half over." That's essentially what he told Peter.

Now, if this were today, would Jesus cook a meal for his disciples? Would he go to their places of business? What would he ask Peter? Would he restore his position as a minister?

We don't know for sure. Even though the details would be different if Jesus lived in America today instead of in Palestine 2,000 years ago, his basic belief that reconciliation is possible would still be the same.

www.ingramcontent.com/pod-product-compliance
Lightning Source LLC
Chambersburg PA
CBHW071009160426
43193CB00012B/1978